Examining multiple theoretical traditions and diverse policy domains, Renée Heberle illuminates historical and contemporary feminisms as complex transformative projects that challenge entrenched assumptions and established ways of being and forge new ways of thinking, new ways of living, and critical contestation over the nature and scope of knowledge and justice. At a moment when male domination and white supremacy are regrouping, this book is a most timely intervention.

Mary Hawkesworth, *Distinguished Professor Emerita of Political Science and Women's, Gender and Sexuality Studies, Rutgers University*

I0023490

FEMINISMS
THE BASICS

This introduction presents, in a readable, lively style, an overview of feminism as an essentially contested field of theory and political engagement. Renee Heberle offers readers a unique approach to studying feminisms in the plural, combining historical and theoretical perspectives on the academic and political lives of the term "feminism." While the popular imagination identifies feminism in the singular with political activity about women's rights, this book introduces readers to diverse, historically significant, critical perspectives and interventions, demonstrating the ongoing relevance of feminisms to contemporary political thinking and practice. This book will be particularly useful in upper-division undergraduate classrooms and introductory courses at graduate level.

Key features:

- Reviews the historiography of the term "feminism" and perspectives and activism associated with the term.
- Introduces feminisms for their value in understanding dynamics of domination and power from interdisciplinary perspectives.
- Explains differences among self-identified feminists as thinkers and activists historically and contemporarily.
- Serves as a springboard for classroom discussions of the nature and purpose of feminisms as complex and contested theories and practices.
- Discusses contemporary work by Brittney Cooper, Sarah Ahmed, Nivedita Menon, and Veronica Gago to set up questions about how/why each contemporary author identifies as a feminist and what they describe as feminism.
- Shows how integral feminisms are to institutions and public understandings of historical and contemporary events and dynamics.

Feminisms: The Basics is a fresh introduction to our understanding of feminisms and feminist theories.

Renee Heberle is Professor of Political Science at the University of Toledo. She co-directs the interdisciplinary major Law and Social Thought and is affiliated faculty with the Department of Women's and Gender Studies. She was the coordinator for the Inside-Out Prison Exchange program at the University of Toledo from 2010 to 2024. Her research interests focus on feminist political theory, state violence, and sexual violence. Her publications include *Theorizing Sexual Violence*, co-edited with Victoria Grace (Routledge, 2009), and *Feminist Interpretations of Theodor Adorno* (Penn State Press, 2006). She has published several essays about sexual violence in feminist journals *Signs: A Journal of Women and Culture* and *Hypatia: A Journal of Feminist Philosophy*, and in the *Oxford Handbooks* on *Gender, Sex and Crime* (2014) and *Feminist Theory* (2016). Her most recent work, "Can Masculinity Survive the End of Sexual Violence?", is included in Gaby Zipfel, Regina Mühlhäuser, and Kirsten Campbell (eds.), *In Plain Sight: Sexual Violence in Armed Conflict* (University of Chicago Press, 2019).

THE BASICS

The Basics is a highly successful series of accessible guidebooks which provide an overview of the fundamental principles of a subject area in a jargon-free and undaunting format.

Intended for students approaching a subject for the first time, the books both introduce the essentials of a subject and provide an ideal springboard for further study. With over 50 titles spanning subjects from artificial intelligence (AI) to women's studies, *The Basics* are an ideal starting point for students seeking to understand a subject area.

Each text comes with recommendations for further study and gradually introduces the complexities and nuances within a subject.

For more information about this series, please visit: www.routledge.com/The-Basics/book-series/B

FEMINISMS
THE BASICS

Renee Heberle

Routledge
Taylor & Francis Group

NEW YORK AND LONDON

Designed cover image: Getty Images

First published 2026
by Routledge
605 Third Avenue, New York, NY 10158

and by Routledge
4 Park Square, Milton Park, Abingdon, Oxon, OX14 4RN

Routledge is an imprint of the Taylor & Francis Group, an informa business

Library of Congress Cataloging-in-Publication Data
Names: Heberle, Renée, 1962– author
Title: Feminism : the basics / Renee Heberle.
Description: New York, NY : Routledge, 2026. | Series: The basics |
    Includes bibliographical references and index.
Identifiers: LCCN 2025026355 (print) | LCCN 2025026356 (ebook) |
    ISBN 9781032206820 hardback | ISBN 9781032206813 paperback |
    ISBN 9781003264682 ebook
Subjects: LCSH: Feminism
Classification: LCC HQ1155 .H47 2026 (print) | LCC HQ1155 (ebook) |
    DDC 305.4209—dc23/eng/20250713
LC record available at https://lccn.loc.gov/2025026355
LC ebook record available at https://lccn.loc.gov/2025026356

ISBN: 978-1-032-20682-0 (hbk)
ISBN: 978-1-032-20681-3 (pbk)
ISBN: 978-1-003-26468-2 (ebk)

DOI: 10.4324/9781003264682

Typeset in Times New Roman
by Apex CoVantage, LLC

CONTENTS

PREFACE

The title of this book does not precisely capture its spirit, though the book is written for those not deeply familiar with feminisms. When encouraged to study the "basics" to learn about an unfamiliar area of scholarship, the implication is that there is a foundation upon which something else is built. However, rather than boiling feminisms down to essential, shareable tenets or to a systematic structure of thought, this book shows instead how feminisms emerge, erupt, divide, process, and act in the world, disrupting and changing the normative status quo in important ways.

That said, readers will come away with a "basic"—in the sense of an introductory and far from exhaustive—understanding of the challenges feminists take up. Readers will be confronted with the complexities of making sustainable changes in thinking and practice about lived experiences and dynamics that feminists find to be unjust. Identifying and undoing damage done by entrenched relationships of dominance and oppression is complicated, as is envisioning alternatives.

This book focuses on what over the last 150 years has been identified as "feminism" and "feminist" by those who write and practice as feminists. It does not say what "feminism" is or should be. My intent is to familiarize readers with many different arguments developed by feminists. Of course, my perspective informs the content, as I have necessarily been selective about what to address. However, my hope is that readers, by way of this book, will find inspiration—whether they are annoyed, angered, surprised, puzzled, or affirmed in their beliefs—to dig into the bibliographical resources and beyond. My purpose is to motivate readers to deepen their understanding beyond what I can say about the phenomenal work referenced and elaborated on herein.

bell hooks famously titled one of her books *Feminism is for Everybody*.[1] She argued that feminism is not just about "women" or any particular time or subject matter in history. Feminism will make the world better for everyone if we listen, read, think, and engage as feminists. I agree with the spirit of her claim—part of me wants everyone to be a feminist; but I also think that feminisms are not for everybody in the sense that there is a lot to disagree with, to challenge, to question, and to build on. I would say instead that feminisms are here to stay, woven into the fabric of the human condition (like it or not!); and that independent and thoughtful engagement with the history that has been made and changed because feminists have written and acted, and the insights available because feminists have thought and critiqued, is key to understanding contemporary conditions and thinking about how to become better than we are.

It is the case that the term "feminism" inspires reaction more often than thoughtful responses. It touches chords of what it means and feels like to be human that some insist should be left in major keys; it renders these chords dissonant, inspiring uncertainty, which scares people. Feminisms are inherently political; they spark conflict where prior there was acceptance or resignation or comfort in the familiar. As a teacher, the only thing I find students have a harder time talking about, depending upon their race, gender, and background, than "feminism," is race. All the more reason to talk, I say. And we begin.

I hope this book contributes to the project of building engagement with feminisms. Friedrich Nietzsche (not a feminist but certainly constructively engaged by feminists) said, "Only that which has no history can be defined."[2] Feminism cannot be defined, pinned down, or stopped. It will continue to make history, and I think readers will see in this book why it is so important to know something about feminisms, in the plural.

---

[1] hooks, bell, *Feminism is for Everyone* (South End Press, 2000).
[2] Nietzsche, Friedrich, *On the Genealogy of Morals* II 13 (Vintage, 1989).

ACKNOWLEDGMENTS

This book practically wrote itself because of the decades I have spent discussing, writing about, and reading about feminisms with others. Thank you to Patricia Jagentowicz Mills for introducing me to feminisms and critical theory. Thank you to Ann Ferguson for furthering my knowledge and supporting me as I entered academia as a feminist scholar.

The Feminist Political Theory Conference, held annually at the Western Political Science Association meeting, has kept me current and engaged with feminisms and feminist scholars. Thank you to Shane Phelan for dreaming and acting it into existence and for including me in the inaugural conference in 1996. The Conference has been an intellectual home for so many of us for almost three decades now.

Thank you to Mary Hawkesworth and Tim Kaufman-Osborn for inviting me along on projects and supporting my work. Mary and Tim are role models and supportive colleagues but, more importantly, very good friends to me. Thank you to Lisa Disch for alerting me to this project and encouraging me to follow up!

Elizabeth Wingrove is a friend and colleague who is essential to my wellbeing as an academic and human. Her generosity in spending time on early versions of some of my essays has made me a much better writer.

The University of Toledo Research and Fellowship program generously supported this work over the summer of 2023. For that I am grateful. I also want to acknowledge that the University of Toledo, now under great pressure to do otherwise, has supported many (let's say) unconventional projects and classes colleagues and

I have come up with over the years. Let us keep our universities and colleges places where we defend and enact academic freedom and work together toward better futures.

Natalja Mortensen and Charlotte Christie encouraged and supported this work as editors. Much gratitude also to copyeditor Carolyn Boyle for her perceptive and detailed work in polishing the manuscript.

Thank you to Bill and Hannah. You are the most precious people in my life.

"I AM NOT A FEMINIST BUT . . ."

INTRODUCTION

When I was a member of the board of a domestic violence shelter in Massachusetts in the early 1990s, I asked my colleagues whether they identified with feminism. They responded, "We do not call our work 'feminist' because we do not want to be controversial or divisive."

The reputation of "feminism" has waxed and waned since the term was first used in 1892 in France to name an organized effort to win equal rights for women. The meaning and significance of the term have also shifted radically over time. While the kinds of thought and activism we might now identify as feminist have been generated and organized for centuries around the globe, for the most part, participants did not identify what they were doing as feminist. For example, in the decades following World War I, women around the globe won the right to vote after a century of organizing and struggle that was not commonly named as "feminist." Rather, in the US and most other places, it was identified as the "suffrage movement" or "the women's rights movement." Nonetheless, this long-lived, complex battle for the vote (which often included other policies and social conditions identified as problematic for women) is now commonly referred to as "feminist." This appellation has contributed to feminism becoming intuitively identified as a rights-seeking movement for women as individuals and equality for women with men—aspirations identified with the tradition of liberalism. However, as we will see, forms of feminism have proliferated; use of the term has never referenced only liberal ideals or values. Hence the pluralization of the term in

DOI: 10.4324/9781003264682-1

the title and the chapters of this book. Further, while my colleagues at the shelter were concerned about feminism(s) as controversial and divisive, this book contends that it is its controversial quality that makes feminism so important and effective. As Martin Luther King argued about non-violent direct action generating creative tensions necessary for injustice to be seen and changed, feminisms generate tensions as they persistently pursue gender justice. In this chapter, I introduce readers to the history of the term "feminism" and to the vastly differentiated systems of domination and injustice confronted by those who identify as women. As for feminisms being divisive, this is a more complex question that I discuss throughout the book.

After World War I, in the Anglo-US world and across the globe, "feminism" as a descriptor for all kinds of struggles waged by and for women lost traction until the 1960s. Since the 1960s, women commonly began to identify themselves, their critiques of male dominance and patriarchy, and their modes of resistance as feminist. In the 1990s, with discourses and practices of neoliberalism dominating discussions of political thought and activity, "feminism" again waned as a descriptor for what women (and men) were doing in the name of gender justice. It was common to hear from diverse places, "I am not a feminist but . . . I believe women should have equal opportunities and should be paid equally to men for the same work." Or, "I am not a feminist but . . . women and girls should be better protected from sexual abuse." In the popular imagination, "feminism" was too sweeping, too "judgmental" (a claim I will return to) in its criticisms and claims; and, for those concerned about ethnocentrism, too Western in its founding principles. "Feminism" since the 1960s went "too far," it was said. If limited to policy prescriptions related to liberal ideas about equality and rights, feminists were considered more "reasonable."

Since about 2010, explicit identification with feminisms by thinkers and activists—now commonly pluralized as in the title of this book—has seen a sharp upswing. This book reviews and offers an assessment of themes in just a few of many recent books identifying themselves as feminist and making claims about feminism(s). For example, with the massive numbers of women and girls speaking out through the global #MeToo movement, the ubiquity of sexual abuse has become clearer and more commonly discussed in the public sphere than ever in history. The insights and histories of feminism and feminists are being rethought and revived.

WHAT IS FEMINISM?

> I myself have never been able to find out precisely what feminism is: I only know that people call me a feminist whenever I express sentiments that differentiate me from a doormat.
>
> Rebecca West[1]

> Feminism is, at its simplest, the belief that gender should not be a reason for any kind of discrimination.
>
> Margaret Thomas[2]

> My feminism will be intersectional, or it will be bullshit.
>
> Flavia Dzodan[3]

The first quotation above defines "feminism" very broadly. Though it is deployed as an epithet meant to label or marginalize her, Rebecca West instead moves to the offensive, claiming feminism as that which empowers/qualifies her to speak for herself and others specifically as a woman and an equal to her interlocutors. The second quote narrows the scope of feminism to a particular policy imperative. Margaret Thomas defines "feminism" as that which is opposed to gender discrimination. This implies it could refer to inflictions of unjust harm against women or men. The third quote by Flavia Dzodan challenges Thomas; it is an assertion of principle about the limitations of feminism when it singles out gender, defined as the difference between men and women, as the problem for feminism to address. As different as they are, each of these claims—feminism as empowerment, feminism as anti-discrimination, feminism as intersectional—represents something critical and accurate about feminism. There are innumerable other assertions about what feminism is, some of which are discussed in this book. For now, however, I will just note from these quotations we can see that feminism is an essentially contested field of analysis and action. It should be referenced in the plural—hence the title: *Feminisms: The Basics*.

I borrow the phrase "essentially contested" from a paper presented by philosopher W. B. Gallie titled "Essentially Contested Concepts."[4] While some refer to feminism as an ideology (an "ism" among other "isms" like liberalism, socialism, and so forth), and others refer to it as a concept or organizing framework for multiple and differentiated ideas and actions, I will refer to it as a "field" of thought and activity. Like Gallie's "essentially contested concepts," feminism generates persistent disputes about the proper use of it as a referent for ideas and actions. We will see, as Gallie argued about essentially contested concepts, this is not a flaw of feminism but a feature and a strength.

Feminism is described here as a "field" rather than an ideology or concept because it is more usefully imagined as a space of theory and action that changes over time than a static object to be defined. Feminist spaces are unsettled and unsettling, for those who identify as feminist and in relation to those who do not. They are at times intensely conflictual, agonistic, and, as such, deeply political. Gallie understood the essentially contested quality of concepts in a neutral way; he argued that basic disagreements as to the meaning of "democracy," for example, produced further insight and knowledge. We will see that feminism as an essentially contested field of thought and action is riven with power relationships, dynamic resistance, inequalities, and privilege; thus, feminism is never "neutral"—it is political "all the way down." It is political in the sense of its internal disagreements and debates, and in terms of its impact and how it generates responses in the contexts and conditions from which it emerges. As we will see in this book, it is feminism's quality as an internally unsettled discursive and practical terrain that sustains its influence; that keeps it alive and kicking across time and space. It is "divisive," but in a good way.

This book reviews theory and action that have been identified with and as "feminist," and argues that the way to learn about feminisms is to study those who think, identify, and act as feminists as they contest the way political, cultural, economic, and social life is organized through gender, sex, and sexuality. This book shows that while feminism in the singular remains commonly identified with rights and equality for women, it accrues different meanings, as the ways in which gender, sex, and sexuality are lived and experienced are contested in different contexts.

From anti-colonial agitation and the woman's rights movements of the 19th century through arguments about the category of "woman" itself, references to "feminism" shift and change.

WHEN DID THE WORD "FEMINISM" COME INTO USE?

As scholars work to recover and claim the significance of women's political activity, we are doing feminist history as defined in the present moment. However, those we study did not act as "feminists" even while they acted in the name of women and toward (depending upon the scholar's perspective and argument) what we might assess as progressive change. It appears obvious, but it is important to remember that feminism is not just any work done with reference to gender or the wellbeing of women. As I discuss, there are non-feminist and anti-feminist movements that claim to serve the interests of women as women. And there are women's movements that avoid identifying as feminist even while they appear in sync with feminist claims and purposes.

Further, we will often see various thinkers identified as feminists. Plato[5] and John Stuart Mill,[6] for example, are commonly referred to as feminists. That they were male is not the relevant question. However, it is one thing to read Plato through a feminist lens and another to call him a feminist. Until the last 50 years, Plato's radical argument that the differences between males and females are irrelevant to their respective capacities to rule as philosopher kings and queens was hardly noticed in the thousands of interpretive treatments of his work. When self-identified feminist scholars began to place the question of gender at the center of interpretive work on the "canon" of Western political philosophy, Plato posthumously became a (prototypical) feminist. Similarly, a search of the classic text, now identified with liberal feminism, *The Subjection of Women*, will find no reference to the term "feminism." Yet, deeply influenced by Harriet Taylor, John Stuart Mill systematically took down every kind of claim that women should be legally and politically subjected to the rule of whatever male was most closely related to them. Mill not only wrote about but consistently acted on his arguments for the equality of women in his personal and political life.

We also hear about "waves" of feminism in the US—the first wave being identified as the 19th century suffrage movement, the second with women's liberation in the 1970s, and a third and fourth associated with generational differences, queer, and transnational feminist movements. Again, these are sometimes retrospective appellations of the term to movements that did not identify as feminist. Suffragists did not call themselves feminists and some queer thinkers and activists consider their work to be about sexuality, not gender—a domain they consider to be of concern to feminists.[7]

It is worth noting that the naming of a social/political activity or movement is a double-edged sword. It can bring people who otherwise feel scattered or isolated together with a sense of solidarity. It can render those who identify as such a target. Or it can marginalize the work by "including" it, while placing it organizationally and discursively outside of mainstream spaces in institutions like workplaces, government, or educational institutions. The identification of activity and theory enacted and written and spoken in the name of gender justice has had these effects over time. It is, therefore, worth reflecting not only on the reputation of feminisms, but—even when "accepted" as a legitimate critique and activity—on where and how feminisms emerge in different forms and in different spaces in the world.

The term "feminism" came into active use after 1891–1892, when women organizing in France called themselves the "*Féderatione Françaises des Sociétés Féministes*" and organized a convention about women's rights in Paris using the term "feminist" in the title. It was not until 1910 that activists in the US began to describe their work as feminist. Further, as argued throughout this chapter, what "feminism" referred to differed across time and space. For example, the cooperation and clashes between a thriving socialist movement and an emergent feminist movement continue to define much of how "feminism" is understood in France. Feminists identified "women's work" as labor, not "merely" reproductive and "natural." They insisted that socialism could and should emancipate women from drudgery in the home and in the workplace by collectivization of otherwise privatized duties of mothering and housework. Backlash from the socialist left was harsh even while French feminists identified as socialist.

Feminist historians Karen Offen[8] and Nancy Cott[9] show that the use of the term "feminism" to describe work related to women's emancipation did not mean it became a unifying or even an "umbrella" term. It has come into play internationally as women have organized in very different contexts in the name of sexual and bodily autonomy; of political, social, and human rights; and of economic equality. There are themes that can be traced through otherwise differentiated efforts to transform the political through the intervention and inclusion of those identified and who identify as women.

For example, critical thinking and activism around the kind of labor women do—by custom, habit, "choice," or under threat—has deeply informed feminisms over time. Nancy Cott, in elaborating what she calls "the birth of feminism" says:

> Feminism [in the US] was born ideologically on the left of the political spectrum, first espoused by women who were familiar with advocacy of socialism and who, advantaged by bourgeois backgrounds, nonetheless identified more with labour than with capital and hoped for the elimination of exploitation by capital and the intervention of a democratically controlled state.[10]

This description illuminates the connections between class and gender in the context of winning the vote; suffrage was not "just" about women but about how socialist values, including reasonable work hours and wages, informed feminist organizing in its earliest days. It is well established how integral the movements to abolish slavery as an institutionalized and legal form of labor and the 20th century civil rights movements were to paving pathways for women to enter public spaces, thus undermining the "ideal woman" or Victorian era ideals as to successful femininity. The influence of class-based analysis and anti-capitalist agitation in the first decades of the 20th century are less familiar but no less important. That "feminism" emerged on the "left" of the political spectrum might seem obvious, yet it should invite active reflection as principles and values ultimately constitute political argument. The principles and values of feminism emerged in complicated relationships to race and class-based movements at the turn of the century in rapidly industrializing countries.

Cott also argues that the feminists of the 1910s in the US worked against the limits of the sexual morality with which suffrage activism was infused since its beginnings in the pre-Civil War era. The generational shift among white women as self-identified feminists in the 1910s and 1920s pushed the boundaries of marital commitment through paving paths away from the marriage imperative and sexual purity. As I discuss in later chapters, from its earliest emergence as a political reference, feminism was identified with sexual autonomy and experimentation.

INTERSECTIONALITY AND GLOBAL FEMINISM

Feminism and feminists have traveled along and across many trajectories over the last 140 years. One question raised on these travels is whether "gender" can be usefully teased out of the complex web of power relations in which it is always already woven as we seek gender justice. The consensus among many contemporary feminists is a resounding "no." Another question is whether and how references to "woman" or "women" are salient considering the first challenge. This begs the question of whether feminism is anything at all if we agree that it should not be grounded in a reference to "women" as they exist in relationships to "men," which is an intuitive way to describe gender and gendered relationships of power.

Feminisms have been entwined with many different historical and social and political movements that involve women. Cott argues that "Feminists [in the 1910s in the US] offered no clear definition of what 'woman' was; rather they sought to end the classification of "woman."[11] She further argues that feminists opposed specialization by sex (difference from men), giving rein to individualism while still relying on a solidarity passed down from the single-issue suffrage coalition that ultimately drew in women and men from all walks of life. She calls this a paradox, showing that individualism and the call to organize women as women are in tension. However, she says the movement of feminism in the 1910s "flourished as much because of as despite its paradoxes."[12] Cott's historical treatment of feminism in the US argues it thrives because of the irreconcilable tensions produced as identities, principles, and strategies are carved out as pathways to public influence and successful claims-making. She does not approach her history as a description of women's subordination to men and what they did about it. She approaches it as a history in which women's and feminists' entry into the public space was always already part of the landscape of politics, making, not merely responding to, history.

We might compare what Nancy Cott says about feminism in US history with what Myra Marx Ferree in *Global Feminism*[13] says about feminism in a collection about global feminism. (Unlike what I do in this book, these thinkers refer to "feminism" in the singular.) Ferree introduces her book with the claim that "Activism for the purpose of challenging and changing women's subordination to men is what defines 'feminism.'"[14] Ferree then discusses the differentiated ways women's movements have or have not been feminist, defined by the purpose stated here: to challenge women's subordination to men. What, then, does one do with the century of struggle among feminists to address class-based, racialized, ability-focused, or labor issues for persons identified as women? How, then, to define "women's" freedom as such—is that freedom always only "from" subordination? Or is it also about struggling for freedom with persons who are men, if those men share women's subordination to colonization or racist regimes? Is it also about class as articulated through gendered dynamics? These are questions Ferree's analysis asks us to address, even while conclusions will be elusive.

Alongside struggle for the vote across the world, women's and feminist movements into and within public spaces, politics, culture, and the waged and salaried workplace took many varied forms throughout the 20th century.

THE DIFFERENT IMPACTS OF INDUSTRIALIZATION AND COLONIZATION

While many identify the 19th century woman's rights movements in the US and Europe as "feminist"—even calling it the "first wave" of feminism, as noted—the word itself did not have much purchase among writers and activists themselves until the 1890s. Thinkers and organizers working toward gender equality and rights throughout the 19th century in the US and Europe, for example, referenced "the woman question," "the question of 'woman,'" and "woman's rights." References to "the ladies" and "sisterhood" also underwrote what have become identified as feminist claims in the 19th century in the West.

"The woman question" emerged in the Victorian era (1840–1914) in England in response to strict legal and ideological restrictions as to the distance and distinction between the private and public spaces and which gender properly inhabited each. The "ideal woman" of this era had white skin, was married and middle class, preferably bore children, and engaged with organizing a household in which she had moral, but no economic or legal, authority. The common law regime that enforced these terms was called "couverture." Under this regime, the legal identity of each woman is subsumed in the legal identity of the male figures upon whom she is dependent (father, brother, spouse). It was a historical enforcement mechanism for the premise that "woman" is naturally unsuited to own property and govern herself according to her own interests within the context of the liberal rule of law. Feminist historians reference these rigid expectations of women and girls the "cult of true womanhood." It was an ideal imposed on all women but a reality for only a few—and even those few fit the mold only imperfectly. Nonetheless, this version of femininity was generally sustained in the context of the "civilizing mission" of modernity in the 19th-century West. The intellectual and protest work women did to empower themselves by way of the vote and independence from male authority was done in relation and resistance to its normative power.

Advocates for women's rights and equality posed the difficult question as to what an "independent woman" would be and do. How would her presence in politics impact the civil order of things? These were mysteries and questions only because the version of the social contract that undergirded the emergence of the nation-state in the West specifically did not include those identified as women as citizens (see Chapter 2 for a discussion of the social contract). She would invent her own pathways into the public space where citizenship mattered; this process of invention would prove to be fraught with disagreement about strategies and identity. Were women militant outsiders threatening to undermine the status quo? Or were they reliable, if excluded, partners in refining the terms on which progress could be made for humankind? Were the qualities that defined femininity to be brought into the public space or were they themselves to be transformed either to fit in with or through the challenge they issued to norms of public behavior in law, the economy, and politics?

"The woman question" would not resonate in the same way in places that did not live under the common law regime of couverture or recognize the rigid distinctions of the public and private spaces which emerged with industrial capitalism in liberal-democratic European countries and the US. This means also that feminist histories of activity by women and on the part of women will be radically differ-ent across the globe. Feminist scholars are not uncovering the status of a universal object of interest called "woman" but a history of the changeable category of gender as it is organized in diverse and com-plicated ways. Every society has a version of gender (the difference between those identified as men and women) that organizes exis-tence; but those versions differ radically. Feminists have distin-guished among references to male/female as biological categories, men/women as sociological categories, and masculinity/femininity as cultural categories. Yet these dualities may be themselves reduc-tionist given the variations of and resistance to these binary distinc-tions extant around the globe. Gender exists everywhere but with significant differences that render any generalizations suspect.

In 1929, Ubakala women of the eastern state of what is now Imo in Nigeria waged war against colonial administrators. Referred to as a "riot" by the colonizers, it is better understood as a rebellion against intrusive colonial administrative measures. The rebellion was a response to the extension of local census taking and taxation to women. While men had been counted and taxed by British colonial administrations, women had been excluded until 1928, when a local schoolteacher was tasked by British administrators with counting (not yet taxing) women and livestock in his district. Women responded by "sitting on the man" or performing dance-play at his compound, preventing him from engaging in his everyday activi-ties. When this did not, as was expected, lead to an adequate response to their complaints, women used their networks across the district to organize and march on the compounds of warrant chiefs, indigenous administrators of British policy. Ultimately 25,000 women marched; more than 40 women were murdered when colo-nial administrators opened fire on the crowds of women. Ultimately, the warrant chief system was destroyed and the counting and threat-ened taxation were stopped.[15]

This protest signaled the latent power of those identified as women in Ubakala. It did not create new institutionalized powers for women but did activate women to use their influence against colo-nial prerogative. This kind of activism is often identified as "femi-nist," but the women did not use the term to describe what they did. They were not rebelling in the name of radical transformations in the gendered order of things but to fight the colonizing powers that undermined their prerogatives as women in their particular social order. This assertion of women's social and economic autonomy and prerogative against colonial dominance assumed women's difference from men in their communities but not their subordination as women to men. If we examine the history of women's struggles, we can see that this question of how women and men differ in their socially constituted roles and identities informs deeply held commitments to one strategy or another to accomplish gender justice.

As shown in this brief description of the "Women's War" in Ubakala, colonization rendered gender struggles very different than did versions of "modern civilization" in the West referenced above.

As feminists, we learn the histories of what women (and men) have done in the name of gender justice and how women understand their positionality in the context in which they struggle. Feminists thereby persistently counter tendencies toward homogeneity in terms of what it means to work in the name of "women" and/or as a feminist. Women act within varied contextual constraints, using the power and influence available or within reach in any given moment creatively to assert their demands in the moment or for a different kind of future.

Another way of looking at this is to note that, at the turn of the 20th century in the West, fast-paced industrialization and imperial reach across the globe were complicating the legal regime of couverture. In the same era, driven by these changes and demands for "modernization" in Western economies and culture, colonization and resource extraction were disrupting social arrangements in Africa. The forces of industrialization and colonization constituted deep class, race, and ethnic differences among women, rendering the category of "woman" a persistently unstable reference point, requiring caveats, adjectives, and references to time and place. The category of "woman" is politicized, or becomes contested, as structural and normative gender arrangements change across time and place.

WHO SPEAKS FOR OR ABOUT "WOMEN"?

In the US and England, the turn of the 20th century is associated with intense and sometimes violent struggles to extend legal identity and rights, including the franchise, to women. The expansion of suffrage—the formal practice of voting in democratic elections for representatives and on issues of the day—was central only toward the end of the century. This helps us to remember that the vote is only one means by which power is distributed and matters considered to be public in any given social order are resolved. As a focal point in the 19th century, the women's rights and suffrage movement is a deeply researched site that further encourages us to think about the category "woman" and associations with the term "feminism." Debates about the "woman question" in the 19th century were not only about what might happen if those identified as women voted. It was a cultural and social question weighted with economic and political significance. In undoing gendered stereotypes and assumptions, those who demanded responses to the "woman question" were challenging deeply held lived experiential truths about gender identity that appeared as self-evident. This is the case no matter where one finds gender arrangements being challenged. The identity of "woman" was also explicitly and consistently being challenged by those underrepresented in the more visible sectors of the women's rights movements.

In thinking about the meanings of "woman" and women's rights in the 19th century, we should consider the iconic, yet misrecognized, historical speech by Sojourner Truth.[16] Truth was born an enslaved person to a family descended from Dutch immigrants in New York state. Upon her own telling, she "walked away by daylight"[17] from being enslaved after her master refused to adhere to the anti-slavery law passed in New York state in 1827. Truth changed her name from the one given in slavery, Isabella Baumfree, and became a nationally recognized speaker for abolition and women's rights. She was mostly unattached to any established organization or movement but known to many of them. In 1851, she delivered a speech in response to hecklers in an audience at a women's rights convention. Not invited to be on the formal panel, she asked permission to rise and speak.

A false version of this signature speech became so famous it is still printed on posters and t-shirts today and is widely invoked by feminist theorists arguing for intersectional and anti-racist approaches to thinking about "woman" and identity. It says in part:

> Well, chillen, whar dar's so much racket dar must be som'ting out o'kilter. I tink dat, 'twixt de niggers of de South and de women at de Norf, all a-talking 'bout rights, de white men will be in a fix pretty soon. But what's all this here talking

'bout? Dat man ober dar say dat women needs to be helped into carriages, and lifted over ditches, and to have de best place eberywhar. Nobody eber helps me into carriages or ober mud-puddles, or gives me any best place.

And ar'n't I a woman?[18]

Yet Sojourner Truth never said these words. Those words were written by Frances Gage 12 years after the speech was given and became the historical record of the speech. As the speech was being given in Akron, Ohio in 1851, Truth's words were more accurately taken down by a journalist named Marius Robinson, who was friends with Truth. He published them in the *Anti-Slavery Bugle* in 1851, but they were lost to history until recently. They are in part:

May I say a few words? I want to say a few words about this matter. I am a woman's rights. *I have as much muscle* as any man and can do as much work as any man. *I have plowed* and reaped and husked and chopped and mowed, and can any man do more than that? I have heard much about the sexes being equal; I can carry as much as any man, and can *eat as much* too, if *I can get it*. I am as strong as any man that is now.[19]

Truth declared to the mostly middle-class and white audience that a "woman's rights" are not reducible to any monistic meaning of "woman" or even "women." She expressed her conviction that she—of African descent, a former slave, the mother of five children, and an independent worker—already embodied what was being "debated" as "woman's rights." She stood and spoke as a "woman's rights" to be in the world as a citizen doing what humans do in the image of God. Her speech is both a reversal of the terms of traditional patriarchy, as she asserts that "women will put the world upright again," and a challenge to the stereotypical distinctions that make some bodies into "men" and other bodies into "women," as she declares her physical and spiritual power.

The speech is loaded with sarcasm, irony, humor, and bemusement as to why those identifying as men were afraid of women's suffrage. She captures what we now call feminist challenges—though the word was not in use at the time to describe what she said and did. Truth did not "ironically" pose the question of *whether* she was a woman, as the apocryphal story declares. She made the claim of her womanhood implicitly in her speech about rights. And, importantly, her claim about herself "as a woman's rights" was not grounded in what most of her audience thought a "woman" was, in the ideal sense of the homebound wife and mother described above. The recorder of the more accurate version of her speech was the Reverend Marius Robinson, a white male journalist. The person whose version "made history" was Frances Dana Barker Gage, a white female reform movement author. She gave Truth—a Northern independent woman whose first language was Dutch—a deep Southern drawl, writing the speech phonetically, and represented her as just barely out of slavery. This was the victimized and vulnerable "woman slave" legible to northern abolitionists. This distortion of her words and identity served the savior narrative to which white liberals, including feminists, have long been tethered. It also (perhaps more importantly) shows how, without an intersectional approach, without understanding that gender and race cannot be disentangled, reform movements—including feminism—will reproduce the unjust conditions they claim to be transforming.

In the US, women's rights and slavery, then Black Civil Rights and women's suffrage, were the primary terrain on which battles around citizenship and nation building were fought. In England and France—both colonizing nations for which racialized differences were created by way of imperial conquest "in distant lands"—national battles for women's rights were fought out against the background of profound class differences between the emergent "new woman" of the bourgeoisie and the women who worked in the burgeoning industrial sectors. The chasms created by class histories and the fierce opposition by white men already in power rendered the path to expanding the franchise not just fraught and dangerous but often unclear and unpredictable. It was further troubled by colonial tendencies and developing discourses of modernity that identified colonized spaces as "backward," as requiring the help of the colonizer to enter history, which for mainstream rights reform advocates included the franchise and general equality upon liberal/ individualist terms for women.

Feminist historians recount these complications and institutionalized habits of white supremacist thought and action as they argue for intersectional history as the best approach to capturing women's history. Remembering race and class as constitutive of, neither derivative of nor separable from, gendered struggles can help us think about the complex histories of struggles around justice as capturing productive tensions among feminists about the category of "woman" and therefore about feminism. "Women" do not have the same histories, so feminisms will necessarily be diverse in their spirit and claims-making. As Nancy Hewitt points out in her critical analysis of the narrative "From Seneca Falls to the 19th Amendment,"[20] women's claims-making across time and space in the 19th century was not primarily defined by accomplishing the right to vote as a mass. In fact, many women had the right to vote at some point during the 19th century and lost it. Mexican women whose land was occupied by the US upon the close of the Mexican-American War were voters and Native Seneca women's rights were foreclosed as Native men became citizens through property allotment. Others identified the right to vote in the context of economic justice issues as workers.

During the post-Civil War writing and ratification of the 15th Amendment, the fight to excise the reference to "male" taken up by white women did not resonate with Black women recently emancipated from slavery alongside Black men. Elsa Barkley Brown[21] explains that in the struggle over the 15th Amendment that would give all men the right to vote but ignored women, Black women took up the vote as a collective voice for their community. They did not see themselves as "not having the vote" or as having the vote only through men; rather, they mobilized in their own interests as women, in churches and other Black spaces, while interpreting the vote as something that would serve their community even if only male persons were enacting the right. However, upon ratification of the 15th Amendment, Black males became less willing to engage in community solidarity with women, excluding them more often from formal power structures, inspiring Black women to mobilize on their own terms.

Through this discussion of how the term "feminism" emerged in the 20th century, and descriptions of different systems of domination confronted by those who identify as women, what I refer to in the plural as "feminisms" is shown to be a field of productive tensions and sometimes unproductive conflict. This in part is because it reflects the cultures in which it emerges. Women's advocates and feminists are not "outsiders;" no matter where they live or what they do, their thinking and activity are interwoven with the social order they contest and transform. Feminisms thus emerge from these struggles not as inherently unifying movements, but as essentially contested fields of inquiry and action. Feminisms will never settle into determinate modalities of thought or action with clearly measurable successes or outcomes. As we explore feminist thought and action in the following chapters, it will become clear that this is not a problem to be solved. It means feminisms constitute a dynamic and charged field of challenges and possibilities.

NOTES

1 West, Rebecca, *The Young Rebecca: Writings, 1911–1917*, quoted in GoodReads. https://www.goodreads.com/quotes/21052-i-myself-have-never-been-able-to-find-out-precisely

2 Thomas, Margaret, "It's a Man's World," *Singapore Business Journal* (1986). https://www.aware.org.sg/2022/06/its-a-mans-world-margaret-thomas-working-woman/

3 Dzodan, Flavia, "My Feminism Will Be Intersectional or It Will Be Bullshit!" *Tiger Beatdown*, October 10, 2011. http://tigerbeatdown.com/2011/10/10/my-feminism-will-be-intersectional-or-it-will-be-bullshit/

4 Gallie, W. B., "Essentially Contested Concepts" in *Proceedings from the Aristotelian Society* 56, vol. 1 (1956) 167–198.

5 Plato, *Republic* trans. C.D.C Grube (Hackett Press, 1992).

6 Mill, John Stuart, *The Subjection of Women* (Hackett Press, 1988).

7 For a critique of this separation, see Butler, Judith, "Against Proper Objects" in *Differences: A Journal of Feminist Cultural Studies* Vol. 6 2+3 (1994) 1–26.

8 Offen, Karen, "Defining Feminism: A Comparative Historical Approach" in *Signs* vol. 14 1 (1998) 119–157.

9 Cott, Nancy, *The Grounding of Modern Feminism* (Yale University Press, 1989).

10 Cott, ibid. p. 35

11 Cott, ibid. p. 4

12 Cott, ibid. p. 8

13 Feree, Myra Marx, *Global Feminism: Transnational Women's Activism, Organizing and Human Rights* (New York University Press, 2006).

14 Feree, ibid. p. 8

15 Hannah, Judith Lynne, "Dance and the Women's War" in *Dance Research Journal* vol. 14, 1+2 (1981–1982) 25–28.

16 Podell, Leslie, "Sojourner Truth Project." https://www.thesojournertruth project.com/?gclid=CjwKCAiAwc-dBhA7EiwAxPRylIK9eU3P2Xyb6 Ot1eCQ9-S1j36hyN6nIW4jfYpcgo-4WK-L5gsodmhoCPqIQAvD_BwE

17 Truth, Sojourner and Nell Irvin Painter, *The Narrative of Sojourner Truth* (Penguin Classics, 1998) p. 41

18 This version is used, for example, in the Modern History Sourcebook, *Sojourner Truth: "Ain'e I a Woman"* (Fordham University Press, 1997).

19 Podell, ibid.

20 Hewitt, Nancy "From Seneca Falls to Suffrage: Reimagining a Master Narrative in US Women's History" in Nancy Hewitt (ed.) *No Permanent Waves* (De Gruyter Press, 2010).

21 Barkley Brown, Elsa, "Negotiating and Transforming the Public Sphere: African American Political Life in the Transition from Slavery to Freedom" in *Public Culture* vol. 7 (1994), 107–146. https://api.drum.lib.umd. edu/server/api/core/bitstreams/4d70bb39-b134-43e7-b0c1-3a62607d3fea/ content

FEMINIST THEORIES

INTRODUCTION

Many events, historical shifts, and theoretical frameworks have influenced the diverse threads of contemporary feminist theory. Given the size of the field, this chapter is necessarily selective. I hope readers will be provoked to explore further. The chapter begins with a discussion of key feminist thinkers identified with liberal, radical, and socialist traditions. These approaches seek out what women have in common: thinkers in these traditions seek unity and/or a universality of experience and identity, respectively, in the category of the individual, the oppressed, or the exploited woman. I spend time with these approaches because of the significant influence they wield as arguments for a particular identity formation that constitutes the meaning of what it is or should be to be a woman. They have inspired fierce and productive critiques and refusals; arguments and debates inspired by feminists engaged with liberal, radical, and socialist ideas, as fraught as they are, inform the feminisms we see around us today.

I then examine theory developed by feminists of color, feminists working with queer theory, and those contributing to transnational theorizing. These critical thinkers figure differences among women and gendered identities into their thinking rather than aspiring to unity, common experiences, or common interests as grounds to define and establish a more just world.

During its emergence in the late 1960s and 1970s, feminist theorizing in the US and Europe sought to establish what women have in common across time, space, and place, and across race, class, and

DOI: 10.4324/9781003264682-2

sexuality. Arguments about the origin (in the singular) of patriar-chal rule, the source (in the singular) of gender oppression, and the identity/meaning (again singular) of "being a woman" developed into powerful theories of gender dynamics and the possibilities for change. The search for the historical origin and/or the source of women's oppression, and efforts to undo those dynamics—whether they create conditions for the denial of individual personhood, sex-ual autonomy, or the value of women's labor power—sought to establish grounds for unity, thereby mobilizing energies for an emancipated gendered order.

However, unity was not only elusive, but controversial as a goal. For very good reasons that will become clear over the course of this chapter, arguments that seek underlying commonalities triggered critique on the grounds that categorizing "woman" (and thus "man") as an essential identity with common attributes across time and space reproduced the problems feminists were confronting; insis-tence on revaluing gender identity as a binary construction of male/female biology or masculine/feminine cultural norms fails to chal-lenge the problems that this binary model itself creates. Further, what Deborah King[1] would call "monist" thinking—that gender is a singular dynamic detachable from other identity formations that shape women's and men's lives—renders invisible or obscures other axes of dominance and oppression.

Considering the critiques mentioned, I present the feminist theo-rizing I begin with in this chapter as generative, as cracking open otherwise relatively stable theoretical traditions and common-sense assumptions about the significance of gender identity in political theory. The feminist theorists considered introduce a gendered and sexual lens to political life and theory; while their work has limita-tions, it inspires ongoing discussion as to their influence on the present and future of feminisms.

When Catharine MacKinnon published a collection of essays as *Feminism Unmodified*,[2] she sought to articulate a feminism that would not rely on theories or practices outside of feminism's terms of reference. Feminist terms of reference, she argued, are the facts, history, and experience of male dominance. However, her effort became associated with an adjective—"radical," meaning "at the root of," or "a singular cause of"—to describe a particular and con-tested, not a universal or agreed upon, approach to feminist theorizing and acting against the many and varied forms of gendered oppressions. Hence, while we will see in Chapter 5 that many contemporary commentaries on feminism write about it without the use of adjectives, feminisms have often been categorized according to the theoretical traditions with which they engage and/or appear most sympathetic. Several books about feminist theory are organized according to adjectival references; liberal feminism, socialist feminism, radical feminism, postmodern feminism, and several other adjectival feminisms have been carefully described in introductory texts like that of Josephine Donovan[3] and Rosemarie Tong.[4] However, as I show here, feminist theorists are always "thinking otherwise than" traditional Western political theories about how we should organize ourselves as human beings and in relationship to our environments. Feminisms are engaged critically with traditions, not exhaustively described by their relationship to those traditions.

LIBERALISM AND FEMINISM

I start with liberalism because it is a hegemonic set of ideas. By "hegemonic," I mean that it defines the "mainstream" of emancipatory thought and action in many spaces across the globe. Individual rights and equality are generally recognizable references, if not universally avowed or agreed upon. As there are "feminisms" in the plural, there are liberalisms. In this section, I describe some basic ideas introduced by and in the liberal tradition and identify some of the conundrums feminists find themselves in when using liberalism as their framework for struggling toward gender justice.

Zillah Eisenstein[5] and Allison Jagger[6] argue, from different perspectives, that feminism pushes the realization of liberal ideals to its limits. They each argue that, when examined through a gendered lens, liberal political philosophy and practice cannot, on their own terms, emancipate women from patriarchal subordination. Nonetheless, the premises upon which liberalism builds throughout its complex and various iterations over the last three centuries in the West form a baseline against which critical theories—feminist and otherwise—have defined themselves. In what follows, we will see that their insight holds true: that liberalism on its own terms will not emancipate women or men. However, if we fail to understand its terms, we will fail to see how liberalism's globalized "common-sense" aspirations—that is, individual rights and equality of opportunity under the law—persistently distract from and obscure structural issues that sustain and perpetuate injustice. In this chapter, I briefly discuss feminist theory that engages with the social contract tradition in Western political philosophy, from John Locke in the 17th century to Immanuel Kant in the 18th century to John Rawls in the 20th century. I then review feminists who are invested in the liberalisms that put civil liberties at the center of their concern during the 19th century and the latter half of the 20th century.

Liberalism as a set of political aspirations referencing human freedom and flourishing was born out of a struggle over how power and resources were to be distributed upon the transition from feudal and monarchic systems into what became the European nation-state system. Liberal thinkers of the 17th and 18th century are identified with the "Enlightenment," which refers to a period of intellectual, philosophical, and scientific emergence from the theocratic premises of medieval intellectual life and monarchic political rule in the West. Social contract theory laid the groundwork for much of what have become the commonsense ideals and values of liberal democracies in the West. Social contract theorists begin their arguments with narratives about life prior to society/legality, or in the state of nature. They then proceed with arguments about individuality, property, rights, equality, and state power that they maintain will best resonate with and sustain values intrinsic to the state of nature—identified as individual liberty and equality—while mitigating its limits and harms. As Martha Nussbaum puts it, liberalisms formulate conceptions of the individual in nature, who then becomes a subject of and subjected to the terms of political order.[7]

Feminist theorists have engaged the tenets of liberalism in a variety of ways. Feminist critiques of social contract theory note the privileging of property right as founded in the investment of labor in transforming nature into something "useful." They address the deeply gendered associations of property ownership with transforming nature into that which is useful and, ultimately, profitable in a marketplace of exchange. For example, liberalisms invest women's reproductive capacities and mothering with moral value, yet these remain in an "auxiliary" role[8] when organizing and maintaining the polity. In John Locke's[9] view, while women may have moral status in the home and even have some semblance of equality to men in that space, they do not transform nature into something useful or marketable. They therefore have no grounds to claim independent political status, much less ultimate political authority. Classical liberal theories imagine women as rightly ensconced in the patriarchal space of the home—even while most women, if assessed on a global scale, have always done all the various kinds of work attributed to men and more, because they are also engaged in the reproductive and caregiving labor necessary to perpetuate human life. Feminist critiques of liberalism show how women were not simply ignored by social contract theorists but actively situated as necessarily subordinate to those rightfully organizing the political space of governance.

Liberal democracies emerged in relationship to industrial and capitalist relationships of production. Liberalism, no matter the form it takes, cannot be disentangled from capitalism; some feminists who engage with liberal theory argue for the mitigation of the excesses of capitalism by implementing a form of redistributive social welfare that provides individuals resources that make the public and private playing fields fairer and more equitable. In her groundbreaking text *Justice, Gender, and the Family*,[10] Susan Muller Okin elaborates the problem with most liberal theories of justice, from the classical to the contemporary. She highlights the exclusion of the family from arguments about justice. Justice arguments apply to rational or, in Martha Nussbaum's language,[11] capable individuals engaging in the public space of decision-making, while the space of the family remains not just in the shadows as the space presumably producing those rational individuals but absent from consideration at all. Okin's work brings the family into presence as a space in and through which conceptions of justice must be studied and tested and norms and relationships changed accordingly. She further points to public policy that assumes a sexual division of labor, with men in the formal workforce and women tending to the home, even if this is not empirically true for most families. Women have always worked for wages and salaries. And they have worked when giving birth and tending to dependents, whether children or the elderly. None of this latter activity is valued as work or thought to be significant in liberal theories of justice.

Okin argues policies related to family life are essential to the working of a just society. She frames her study of the potential for a just form of the family to be realized by way of critiques of contemporary male-oriented liberal theory that addresses gender and families as footnotes to their vision of how we might achieve a just public sphere. Okin argues we will never achieve a just public sphere if we ignore the injustice in the so-called "private" sphere. Not only is that private space governed by economic and legal principles, and therefore not natural or private in any sense, but it is governed by an ideological commitment to masculinity as the dominant decision-making and public-facing gendered identity. She argues the family is the "linch-pin"[12] of gender; that gender identity formations and dynamics follow from the organization of the family. It is important to note—as Michaele Ferguson recently has[13]— that Okin is not writing about families as they exist in the world, but about the family that is idealized in modernized social orders with a male breadwinner and a female housekeeper and child raiser. This ideal is not the reality or the aspiration for many families, yet policy is designed to incentivize its realization and sanction those who fall short. Thus, the ideal sustains an artificial and unnecessary emphasis in law and policy on an imagined gendered and sexual division of labor which constitutes women as mothers and wives and thus as the subordinate gender.

Okin argues for liberal principles of justice to be brought into the space of the family. She argues for the end of gender, which sounds like a radical claim. However, what she means is the end of gender as an organizing principle of relationships among individuals, not as an identity as such. She engages critically with liberalism, but she does not critique the basic values of property rights, equality, or individuality liberalism presents as organizing principles. Individuals should live as equals in the space we call family, sharing responsibilities and avoiding any semblance of the naturalized patriarchal hierarchies she argues traditional ideas about the family perpetuate. She says this degendering of the familial sphere with respect to roles and responsibilities will benefit men and women and children, leaving in place those identities while reorganizing the terms on which they will engage in doing "families" and recognizing the diverse forms families might take if not constrained by the ideal.

Okin's arguments are radical in the sense that we are far from realizing the policies she suggests will create an egalitarian space for men and women to live together. They are also radical arguments in the formal sense that to be radical is to "get at the roots" of the problem. Okin argues that the organization of the family is the cause, the root, of the oppression of women. Most feminists will agree that the naturalization of women's 24/7 obligation to care for and to do the work of the household is central to the perpetuation of gendered oppression. Detaching and/or releasing men and women from the default gendered roles remains a very difficult nut to crack. Okin's work shows how what liberalism thought was personal should be identified as political, as subject to the terms of justice, given that actual individuals live in families and must necessarily be given choices as to how to live in and with families or not.

Reflecting priorities set out by critics like Okin, feminist activists who engage in liberal forms of advocacy work to change policies about childcare, domestic violence, and workplace discrimination. Insisting upon identifying women as individuals rather than wives and/or mothers has proven helpful and created important policy changes in the context of reproductive rights, domestic violence law and rape reform, and workplace and educational discrimination. Enforcing Title VII of the Civil Rights act, which includes sex in the statutory language but was rarely deployed for women as victims of sexual harassment and other discriminatory workplace practices, was the primary goal of the founders of the National Organization of Women. This is one of the few organizations that has survived the conservative shift and consequent backlash against feminism of the 1980s and 1990s. Its legal defense fund has supported litigation that has led to the reform of laws governing family life, including divorce law, access to credit, and sexual violence in all its forms.

Upon the centenary celebration of passage of the 19th Amendment granting women the right to vote, Marjorie Spruill[14] published an important book looking back at the feminist activism in the 1970s identified with liberal aspirations of rights and equality for women. The late 1960s and 1970s were extremely productive years in terms of statutory reform impacting women's equality. For example, the Equal Employment Opportunity Commission (EEOC) ignored the provision of Title VII of the Civil Rights Act (1964) prohibiting sex discrimination. Feminists pushed hard in the courts

and in Congress, and in 1972 legislation was passed to force attention among EEOC attorneys to these cases. Title IX, which prohibits
discrimination in educational institutions, also passed in 1972. In
the early days, Title IX was applied primarily in the context of girls'
and women's sports, but it has since become far more visible and
controversial in struggles over sexual harassment and violence in
educational institutions.

In 1975, in Mexico City, Mexico, the United Nations hosted an
international women's conference. In the US, Congress then followed up on this landmark event, appropriating $5 million to host a
national women's conference in Houston, Texas. This initiative
funded women to meet over the space of two years in each of the 56
states and US territories to organize a platform and desired outcomes for a meeting to be held in 1977. Over 2,000 delegates
attended, including women from across the ideological spectrum.
Spruill identifies this as a watershed moment in what had become
an "establishment" feminist politics—a politics that was integrated
into systems of power in Washington DC and across the states.
Educational and polemical pamphlets were circulated. Ideological
differences drove sometimes painful debates. The list of priorities
issued by the conference demanded not only equality and rights for
women under law, but substantive attention and resource allocation
to lift material barriers inhibiting women's full participation in the
social and political order. Importantly, the conference supported
immediate passage of the Equal Rights Amendment—an issue that
self-identified anti-feminists, led by Phyllis Schlafly, organized
nationally to oppose, asserting that feminists are merely a small fac-
tion claiming to speak for all women. Schlafly argued the Equal
Rights Amendment would harm women, putting them in danger of
deprivation of alimony in case of divorce, separate public facilities,
and other "privileges" attendant upon being a woman.

These accomplishments and events have been rendered invisible
to the popular consciousness of feminisms in the US, in part because
of the successful campaigns against such efforts like passage of the
Equal Rights Amendment and the slashing of federal programs supporting poor families during Ronald Reagan's conservative presi-
dency of the 1980s. Spruill's history reminds us of what was
accomplished by way of working within a system defined by liberal
values to institutionalize women's rights. Feminism in its liberal

form as a struggle for the lifting of barriers and the substantive granting of rights and equality was a bipartisan effort in many states and at the national level throughout the 1970s. Republican and Democratic administrations were influenced by and responded to feminist advocacy.

As mentioned above, however, feminists wrestle with the inclusion of women in the liberal order given its limitations, its mutually constitutive relationship with extractive and exploitative forms of capitalism, and its assumption that individual rights and liberties take precedence over public goods. Liberalism has not facilitated the end of sexual violence against women, as indicated by the extraordinary outpouring of stories of abuse and harassment inspired by the #MeToo movement that emerged 50 years after the first speak-outs on rape. In the US, where liberalism remains more anti-statist than in other established liberal states, childcare and workplace policies have not relieved women of the second and third shifts of caregiving. Women of color remain at the bottom of the pay scale and particularly targeted in the culture wars. Abortion was declared a constitutional right under the umbrella of privacy rights in 1973. In 2022, the court overturned this precedent, declaring that a right to abortion "cannot be found" in the Constitution. While access was always difficult for women with few resources and limited by multiple state policies, getting an abortion and being pregnant are now extremely high risk for women, medically and legally, across many states. The privacy right that the Supreme Court interpolated from what are known as the penumbras, or conditions for existence, of other rights in the First, Third, Fourth, and Fifth Amendments in the Bill of Rights to decide cases about contraception (*Griswold v Connecticut* 1965) and sexual activity (*Lawrence v Texas* 2003) no longer apply, as a fundamental right of citizenship in the United States, to individuals who become pregnant. They must comply with state laws about where, when, and how they can have the medical procedure of abortion. Individual women—usually white and middle to upper class—are, in the aggregate, better off educationally and economically than prior to the 1970s. However, freedom from violence, the burdens of caregiving, economic hardship, and equality has not been achieved by means of liberal reforms for those who identify as women in general. The alternatives to liberalism that feminists have argued for since the 1970s deepen the analyses available to understand what women are up against in terms of achieving gender justice. Liberal reforms have, at best, brought uneven benefits to women and uncertain victories, given that politics remains a profoundly masculinist space that those who identify as women must still navigate specifically as women.

RADICALISM AND FEMINISM

ACTIVISM AND CONSCIOUSNESS-RAISING

Possibly no form of feminism in the US has been caricatured and ridiculed and critiqued by other feminists more than that identified as "radical" feminism. Radical feminism is identified as such because "radical" means getting to the root. Feminists who identified as radical in this way argued, in various ways, the roots of women's oppression to be sunk deepest in male power or patriarchy. Despite the caricatures and the legitimate critiques, discussed below, feminists who identify as radical have arguably been very effective in forcing recognition of patriarchal dominance in the West, where liberalism so effectively obscures structural relationships of dominance like the public/private split in gendered responsibilities.

The archetypal moment of emergence of radical feminism is the 1968 "bra-burning" protest of the Miss America Pageant in Atlantic City, New Jersey. This protest included a metal trash-burning barrel into which protesters would throw constraining undergarments, high-heeled shoes and other signifiers of feminine "style." In fact, the "bra-burning" that continues to drive the story never happened, as the group did not get a permit to burn on the boardwalk.[15] Nonetheless, word of the protest spread as if it did, becoming a marker in feminist history and a point of departure for the caricatures of those who would become identified as "radical" feminists.

While criticisms of the protestors as "bra-burning, man-hating feminists" were unfounded, legitimate questions were raised about the protests that were taken very seriously by the protestors themselves. For example, they displayed posters of women as if they were slabs of beef cut apart for inspection and portrayed competitors as sheep. In the spirit of self-criticism, feminists theorized a "pro-woman" account of why those competing did so. They insisted the contestants themselves should not be the target of feminist critique. Women enter such competitions to receive recognition and resources by whatever means available to them as women. If women are sexual objects, and if competing as such can lead to a college scholarship (a prize for winning the contest), then we could argue that women are using the best means at their disposal to advance as individual women, even if it is harmful to women as a class. Thus, we must change the terms of a world wherein the means by which women can best flourish is by turning their bodies into sexual commodities.

Another significant form of public protest taken up by radical feminists were "speak-outs" about abortion and rape, which were organized in the early 1970s and continue in many forms today. Taking the phrase "the personal is political" (discussed in Chapter 4) as a guiding principle, radical feminists gave experiences that were the most intimate and private—the decision to end a pregnancy (illegal at the time in most states) and sexual violence—narrative form in public spaces.

Due (again) to bad history, which has over the last 20 years been revised by feminists, and the failure to account for the depth and breadth of theorizing among radical feminists, the movement has been identified as monolithic, "extreme," "man-hating." More thoughtful critics identified radical feminism as "essentialist," which means "the feminine" or woman as such has qualities that must be discovered and liberated for gendered justice to prevail. In focusing on discovery of the liberated *woman* beyond patriarchy, it does not account for race and class in relationship to gender as systems of oppression.

However, we should not minimize the impact of the radical feminist theorizing, protests, grassroots organizing, direct actions, and speak-outs of the late 1960s and 1970s. Changes in law, such as the demand for affirmative (not tacit) consent to be proven by the defense in sexual assault cases, can be traced to radical feminist organizing against sexual violence. Domestic violence taskforces in law enforcement agencies—indeed, the identification of domestic abuse as a crime—can be attributed to radical feminists' insistence that the heteronormative private space is one of domination and submission, not companionate but sometimes mutually conflictual relations.

The language of dominance/submission differentiates radical feminists from feminists more identified with liberalism. The latter argue that the construction of family members as rights bearing will remedy the invisibility of the family in the public sphere. Radical feminists often argued for the abolition of the family as irredeemably oppressive. The politicization of sexuality, inspired by essays such as "The Myth of the Vaginal Orgasm" by Anne Koedt[16] and questions about what it means politically to be lesbian (is it a kind of political boycott of men, an affirmative desire for women that denaturalizes heteronormativity, or both?), would not be what it is today without the influence of radical feminism.

The association of gender oppression with sexuality and sex oppression is a legacy of radical feminist ideas and organizing. Liberal feminists tend to obscure or ignore sex, sexuality, and sexual activity as sites requiring liberation from patriarchal rule. Liberalism will claim a right to consent to sexual activity but not theorize or think about sex as such as potentially liberating. Radical feminists explored and theorized these sites and dynamics in consciousness-raising sessions—spaces where women spoke with one another of otherwise individualized and intimate experiences identified by liberalism as outside the political. Consciousness-raising was the site of theory-making for radical feminism; it was a means by which to expand the scope of "the political" to include what had been "personal."

As the US women's rights movement in the 19th century was shaped by slave abolitionist movements, the most radical versions of feminist theory and activism in the mid-20th century were shaped by women deeply committed to the civil rights and new left student movements of the 1950s and 1960s. The recognition that, in what civil rights activists called "the beloved community," women continued to be identified for purposes of sex and other kinds of service to men motivated some white women to begin to organize "around their own oppression" as women.

THEORIZING FROM EXPERIENCE

From early meetings among women, held separately from men to give participants time and space to speak, radical feminists developed an analysis that male dominance—sometimes referred to as patriarchy—is the root cause of women's oppression as a class. Male dominance, enforced by law and by violence, explains women's condition, not biological differences or socially constructed but complementary gender roles. In contrast to liberal feminism's focus on altering gender roles associated with political, social, and economic dependence through expanding individual rights to women, radical feminists argue that women's dependence is enforced by way of sexualized dominance and threat. Male power will not give way to persuasion or evidence of women's capacity to reason. In this view, women's oppression cannot be "fixed" by extending rights but must challenge the psychological and material foundations of gender identities and heteronormative sexual relationships.

As noted above, the paradox implicit in liberal feminist work—that to become individuated as citizens with rights, women must organize as a "right-less" group—is argued by Zillah Eisenstein to resolve into a radical feminist position. Without changing the fundamental and structural sexed differences between men and women, women will always be the subordinate sex class; they cannot be liberated one at a time as individuals. In this sense, women are a "sex class," not an aggregation of individuals who are oppressed by their ascribed gender roles. But what is meant by "sex class" in radical feminism? Shulamith Firestone[17] and Catharine MacKinnon[18] turn to Marxist methods to respond to this question. They make clear they do not think Marx or his co-author Friedrich Engels were any kind of feminists. Marx and orthodox Marxism dismisses issues of gender, arguing that class identity and the liberation of the working class from capitalist chains would subsequently render women free from the exploitative home created in the interest of the bourgeois class. As Firestone eloquently spells it out:

It would be a mistake to attempt to explain the oppression of women according to this strictly economic interpretation. The class analysis is a beautiful piece of work, but limited: though correct in a linear sense, it does not go deep enough. There is a whole sexual substratum of the historical dialectic that Engels at times dimly perceives, but because he can see sexuality only through an economic filter, reducing everything to that, he is unable to evaluate it in its own right.[19]

For unless revolution uproots the basic social organization, the biological family—the vinculum through which the psychology of power can always be smuggled, the tapeworm of exploitation will never be annihilated. We need a sexual revolution much larger than—and inclusive of—a socialist one to truly eradicate all class systems.[20]

Radical feminists advocate not for equality of men and women in their given gender identities, but for the revolutionary elimination of sexed roles and therefore of gender identity altogether. Firestone was not interested in reforming the political system by opening it up to include women as individuals. To be "radical" was to get at the roots of oppression and she argued the roots were in the biological division of labor organized socially through the family. If the family, organized according to naturalized associations of the biological capacity to gestate and give birth with caregiving—named by feminists as the reproductive division of labor—continues unchanged sex-class oppression will not end. Radical feminists argue generally that sex class is the original system of oppression. All other movements for liberation, particularly the socialist class revolution, can be enveloped in the revolution to liberate women from their sex-class status.

This is, in part, the kind of argument that tangled feminists and left progressives in debates about which system of oppression was the most significant or the most likely, if revolutionized into a liberated condition, to bring others along in its wake.

The contributions of radical feminist theory to subverting sex and sexual norms are powerful and compelling. Firestone brought together Marx/Engels and Freudian analysis, subverting the traditional male-centric logic of those theories, to illuminate how sex and sexuality, not gendered roles, are at the root of female oppression. Gender habits and norms follow, she argues, from the material and psychosocial conditions of the family form. The family cannot be reformed. Rather, one must take the means of reproduction out of the female body and communalize the reproductive means of caregiving (we will see a version of this world imagined by Marge Piercy in her book discussed in the final chapter). This, Firestone argues, will undo any "natural" cause of male/female difference. As a materialist thinker alongside Marx and Engels, she argues technology allows for revolution but only in conjunction with a radical upheaval in women's status as the dependent sex-class.

Firestone was a founder of Redstockings, the organization in New York City that organized the first speak-out on the right to abortion in 1969. Their focus on reproductive "enslavement" and sexual repression was, for radical feminists, a response to what they saw as liberal feminists' concessionary aspirations to equality to men within the oppressive social order men created in their own image and interests.

Catharine MacKinnon—a legal scholar who worked closely with Andrea Dworkin, an anti-violence and anti-pornography activist—synthesized much of what radical feminist thinkers and activists argued during the 1970s and 1980s. In her writing and advocacy, Mackinnon remains identified with the anti-pornography, anti-sexual harassment, and anti-sexual violence movements for social and legal change. While she does most of her activist work in the field of law, her analyses created a profoundly influential framework for how to think about policy writ large.

For MacKinnon, male power defines what is knowable as "woman," "feminine," or "female." Critics argue this analysis strips women of agency, of epistemic capacity (the ability to know themselves or the world), and renders male power monolithic when in fact it is differentiated by race, class, sex, and every other identify formation that differentiates subjects in the material and cultural world.

MacKinnon finds value in Marx's argument that exploitation happens when that which makes us human, that which makes us conscious in and about the world, is taken from us, turned into a commodity outside of our control, and used in exchange relations that do not benefit us. For Marx, labor power (work) is what constitutes us as human. There is no imagined "state of nature" necessary for Marx to understand the emergence of a social order, as there is for social contract theorists. Rather, when "man" first picks up a stick to dig, he is making his own history, consciously transforming nature; this ability distinguishes him from beasts, forging his humanness. Capitalism extracts labor power from workers, paying workers less than that for which they produce is sold to make profits. Adapting Marx's thinking about labor power, MacKinnon says that "sexuality is to feminism what work is to Marxism."[21]

Elaborating on this parallel construction between feminist and Marxist theory, she argues that "Sexuality is the social process that creates, organizes, expresses, and directs desire,"[22] like capitalism does for production. In patriarchy, sexual relationships are not natural or pre-social; they manifest the organized expropriation of the sexuality of some for the use of others. "Woman" is the effect of this. Woman is defined as objectified sex, that which is to be used to satisfy male desire in a male-dominated social order. MacKinnon's claims are, on the face of it, borne out by numbers and a long history of male perspectives defining the terms of sexuality, in court, in homes, in the workplace, and on the street. Her work synthesizes much radical feminist thinking about sex and sexuality as constructed by male dominance. This effort to render women as a "class" of oppressed subjects responds to those who individualize and personalize each moment or experience of sexualized suffering or harm as the fault of pathological males (outliers) or the perspectives of neurotic females (frigid or hysterical). It is also in response to the flipside of this: the dismissal of sexualized suffering or harm as flirtation, as an understandable mistake ("I thought she wanted it"), or failed seduction.

MacKinnon's book *The Sexual Harassment of Working Women*[23] and her legal arguments and advocacy deeply influenced the rendering of sexual harassment as subject to civil actions 20 years after Title VII of the Civil Rights Act of 1964 was passed in Congress. She wrote at a time when sexual violence in all the forms it takes was slowly—under the influence of feminist agitation and influence in many different forms—being understood not as a normal enactment of male entitlement, to women as property in marriage or to women's bodies in the workplace, but as a problem.

MacKinnon shows men write the law from a male perspective which defines woman as other than and subordinate to men. She follows on Simone de Beauvoir's magisterial work *The Second Sex* in arguing that "woman" (and for MacKinnon, all of sexuality) is a product of male dominance.[24]

While the organizing and legal advocacy of radical feminism centered women, the theory and sometimes the practices begged the question of how to think about women's agency, historically and otherwise. If woman is a product of male desire, what were/are *women* doing? Are they merely subordinates? Are they falsely conscious, wanting or even desiring only what is expected by men? Are they always only suffering? The answer given by radical feminism is largely, "We cannot know who or what women are or have been until men get their foot off our necks." That foot is weighted with historically derived political and legal male prerogative backed by sexualized and gendered force. What would women be "beyond" male dominance? What would be an authentic female sexuality? These questions framed the turn to what Alice Echols, among others, calls "cultural feminism." Some feminists made a hard turn to celebrating women's difference rather than, as MacKinnon does, arguing that the difference is created by male dominance and is therefore defined by subordination.

"CULTURAL FEMINISM"

The efforts in the early 1970s and thereafter to "discover" or "reveal" the feminine spirit and/or sexuality and/or character as it might exist before or outside of the patriarchal order were synthesized in a manifesto titled "The Woman-Identified Woman"[25] (WI-W), written collaboratively by the Radicalesbians. WI-W articulates what became identified as a lesbian-feminist argument for a radical turn toward women and away from men, not as a temporary means by which to find one's voice, as in the consciousness-raising model, but as revolutionary vanguardism.

WI-W asserts several different points: (1) that a "lesbian is the rage of all women condensed to the point of explosion."[26] (2) That "lesbian" is an epithet derived from male supremacist ideology to divide women that is successful because women fear being excluded or punished for not being a proper "woman." (3) "Lesbians" exist because male supremacy and heterosexuality exist as norms against which all other desire and behavior is measured. The second point can be argued logically: if, according to patriarchal ideology, a "proper woman" is a female who desires men, lesbians cannot be proper women. Lesbian feminists ultimately embraced this, as Monique Wittig would later—controversially—claim that "lesbians are not women."[27]

It is in the final paragraph of WI-W that we find reference to the "cultural revolution": "It is the primacy of women relating to women, of women creating a new consciousness of and with one another, which is argued to be at the heart of women's liberation and the basis of the cultural revolution."[28]

More importantly, however, the manifesto and other writings by separatist feminists draw out the ways in which people called women, socially constructed or otherwise derived, are embedded with those who are the problem—that is, "men." What was sometimes referred to as "political lesbianism" was an effort to disentangle women from patriarchal influences that go as deep as the womb when the fetus is identified or wished for as a girl or a boy for cultural, social, or economic reasons. This persistent dualist differentiation perpetuates gender and sexuality as hierarchically organized.

The separatist impulse was not limited to lesbian relationships. Many feminists engaged in complex entrepreneurial efforts to create a separate culture. Feminist bookstores, music companies, credit unions, and publishers emerged in the late 1970s. Most did not survive through the turn of the 21st century, but they did contribute to the entry of women as independent economic actors into cultural spaces.

Radical feminism remains profoundly influential, particularly in policy related to sexual violence in all its forms. The "Power and Control Wheel" often seen in domestic violence shelters and arguments about affirmative consent are derived directly from radical feminist arguments about the constitutive dominance of males over females and the demand for recognition of the harms men, as such, inflict on women, as such. As is discussed later, the #MeToo movement, which started in 2006 and went "viral" in 2017 with allegations coming from a vast range of individuals victimized on the basis of sex, sexuality, and gender is threaded with radical feminist arguments about male power and feminized victims. It is a digital version of the speak-outs radical feminists organized to render the personal political in a very public fashion. While sexuality and women as sex objects have always been commodified on the terms of the capitalist economy, sexual violence and abuse are now understood to be properly political and subjects of public policy.

SOCIALISM AND FEMINISM

WOMEN AND CLASS IDENTITY

As noted above, radical feminism emerged from new left movements as women sought to liberate themselves on terms independent from male-dominated political perspectives and theories. From the early imperative to organize separate meetings so women could speak for and as themselves, radical feminists developed sophisticated theories and practices arguing that feminists must focus singularly on male dominance as we seek liberation.

Socialist feminism emerged from but remained in a relationship to developments in Marxism across the 20th century. Socialist feminists showed how women as gendered/sexed beings were misrecognized as not-quite workers in Marxist analysis and practices. While Firestone and MacKinnon used Marx's theory as a kind of model or template that works as an analogy to understand basic themes in feminism (sexuality is to feminism as work is to Marxism), socialist feminists worked to integrate the theoretical and practical insights of feminism and Marxism to understand gendered/sex oppression/exploitation.

Following on a theme of this book, feminists who identify as radical and those who are socialist wish to politicize what liberal capitalism relegates to the non-political private spaces of individual responsibility and family. The space of production, according to liberalism, is not in itself political, but must be protected from political intervention. Market principles should predominate, even while some regulation might be necessary to mitigate their worst effects. The space of the family is also, according to liberalism, not in itself political. It too must be protected from political intervention as a space free of power and shaped by "natural" and/or "social" relationships that fulfill moral and reproductive imperatives.

Socialist theory, while shifting and changing in important ways over the 20th century, is historical and materialist. What does this mean with respect to feminism? Socialist theory pays attention to what human beings do with their bodies and their time more so than to abstractions such as individual rights and equality. It pays attention to our productive lives rather than our lives as cultural or social beings or political subjects of national/state rule. It argues that every human society has had primary means and relationships by which it reproduces and produces itself. As said above about Marxism, it argues that our material productive lives distinguish us from animals, not our mental (reason) or psychological (consciousness) lives. It is historical because men themselves, not God or nature, drive human destiny; as Marx said in *The Eighteenth Brumaire of Louis Bonaparte*, "Men make their own history, but they do not make it just as they please; they do not make it under circumstances chosen by themselves, but under circumstances but under circumstances found, given, and transmitted from the past."[29] It is materialist because it argues politics, society, and culture all follow from the relationships that govern how we make and distribute the stuff we need and want.

So how could women—who, as women, are not understood to be engaged with the primary productive systems of most social orders—fit within this theory? Can women be a "class" if, in their primary roles, their work activities are not directly exploited toward the ends of capitalist profit? If they are mostly engaged, materially and otherwise, in the reproduction of the human race through familial and kinship structures that are outside of the formal economy, how can they be understood in the context of the change-making quality of production, inflected by technological advancement and global mobility? Is it not the case that in advanced capitalism, "women" will disappear into the category of worker with liberal advances in distributing rights to equal opportunities in productive work and the increasing demand for different kinds of labor in the post-manufacturing era? If that is the case, what critical purpose would a woman/gender/sexed theory serve in rendering the world more just as it changes?

One approach socialist feminists take to these questions is to argue that women are not fulfilling natural or moral roles as mothers, sisters, daughters, or wives. Rather, following physiological capacities (giving birth), they are constituted as wives and mothers and then alternatively socialized and forced to do the reproductive work necessary to sustain capitalist production outside the home. To become feminist, as argued by Ann Ferguson in *Sexual Democracy*, women must

> be able to identify with sex class over family class, to be aware of each other as a historically cohesive group, with a common culture and common interests by virtue of our position in the sexual division of labor in the family and in society.[30]

Ferguson elaborates new means by which to identify "class" through racialized and sexualized formations that fulfill several of the criteria, like exploitation and control of resources, that signify class status. Ultimately, she says women will identify either with family class (her status dependent upon the male figure and his status as working or ruling class) or sex class (her status seen as in common with other women dependent upon males for their status).

Ferguson argues that women in late modernity are likely to identify increasingly as a sex class given the changing conditions of
capitalism in relationship to the family. More women are entering
the wage economy and requiring childcare. More women are freer
to divorce even while, upon divorce, their economic status plunges
relative to the male figure and they remain the primary caregivers to
the young and the elderly. As unmarried and primary caregivers,
they are often not qualified for or considered seriously as candidates
for more than low-waged hourly positions.

Despite Ferguson's attunement to racial formations throughout
her book, in a chapter explaining her optimism for women to emerge
as a sex class, Ferguson continues to assume that all women experience the historical shift she describes in women's sex-class status in
the age of dual incomes and increasing aggregate rates of divorce.
However, as Angela Davis shows,[31] Black women and many women
of color around the world have neither benefited from nor been burdened in the same way by what Ferguson labels the capitalist patriarchal nuclear family. Feminists who are women of color have
shown, for example, how patterns of work and family in diasporic
communities in the US and Europe are shaped by the history of
colonization and immigration; while patterns of work and families
in the Black community are shaped by the legacy of slavery, which
forbade nuclear family formations and, in its aftermath, undermined
through violence and economic deprivation the best efforts of
ex-slaves to find their families or create new financially stable families. The histories and material production of the familial form are
not the same for all women; the model of sex-class identification
over family class identification assumes a commonality of familial
forms as oppressive across time and space.

Allison Jaggar[32] addresses how feminists have engaged with Marx
and Marxism to develop socialist feminist theories. She contrasts
these with liberal and radical feminist theories, which she argues are
inadequate to the task of liberating women as such. Liberal feminism
focuses on women becoming individuals (rather than wives, mothers,
sisters, daughters, sex objects, or breeders) and fighting for fairer
terms on which to enter public spaces of political, economic, cultural,
and social influence. Anti-discrimination battles, fought primarily
through the courts, and affirmative equality (comparable pay and
family leave) campaigns characterize liberal feminist politics.

Radical feminists focus on women as a universally oppressed sex. They use the language of class but in the sense that the nature of sexed oppression is grounded in male sexual dominance, which is cultural and psychic and backed by sanctions ranging from economic deprivation and oppression to hidden forms of violence like rape, domestic abuse, and harassment; radical feminists define the problem as the investments of male power in setting the terms of all gendered and sexed interactions. Separatism, as described above, is considered key to finding out who women authentically are beyond their coerced intertwinements with a male-dominated world.

Socialist feminists argue that as economic subjects, women are both like and not like men. Recasting what women do in the home is a primary focus. What Ann Ferguson calls sex-affective labor (care and love of family members) and the actual work of cleaning, cooking, and organizing life in the household characterize women's contributions to the society that Marx presumed to be built only in and by those engaged in the formal waged economy. Women's contributions are not always experienced as coerced or exploitative, but only because they are "naturalized" by way of the historically gendered division of labor. What Jaggar calls the "science" of socialist feminism shows that women's activities and work are necessary to the capitalist order and therefore part of the problem to be solved on the way to revolution and liberation.

Socialist feminist activism includes the "wages for housework" campaigns. In 1972, Sylvia Federici helped organize the New York Wages for Housework Committee. The organization spread beyond New York during the 1970s. "Autonomy from men is Autonomy from capital that uses men's power to discipline us [women]."[33] This quote speaks to how the wages for housework campaign linked feminism and socialist critiques of capitalism. The key to this campaign was in the opening of the "private" space to materialist critique, but also in the recognition that wages for housework is a demand that is impossible for capitalism to meet. That impossibility means that to "win" this campaign, political economy will have to be reinvented beyond the public/private, formal/informal, instrumental/love dichotomies liberalism invented to support capitalist production. In the 2018 interview in the *Boston Review* cited above, Federici identifies wages for housework campaigns as strategies of refusal. What would happen if all women ceased to do the work that women are resigned/consigned to? The pamphlet linked above gives some idea. It is hard to imagine, as indicated by the paucity of fictional representations of such a strategy in writing, film, or music.

Wages for housework, inspired by socialist feminist critique, assumes (as do liberal and radical feminism) that women have something fundamental—in this case, the kind of labor they are expected and often forced to perform—in common as women. Again, with references to Black women and women of color, feminists engaged with socialist theory acknowledge that historical experiences are different but consider those differences to be epiphenomenal (superficial). They argue for us to see "woman" as a sex class potentially unified in struggle against a system that oppresses her.

Feminists of color, including but not limited to Black and Latina and Asian feminists, have asserted their difference from white women as fundamental, not contingent or something to be moved beyond as the real struggle for equality and/or the revolution advances. Allison Jaggar says in her introduction to *Feminist Politics and Human Nature*, cited above, that in highlighting differences (in this case among liberal, radical, and socialist feminisms), she intends to resolve those differences through her theory and suggestions for practice. In fact, when she discusses how she will include Black feminists and women of color feminists in her work, she says she will do so only insofar as they have engaged with liberalism, radical feminists, and/or Marxism, not because she is learning from them as feminists of color. Ultimately, she wishes to show that socialist feminism is the unifying theory and practice.

STANDPOINT THEORY AND FEMINISM

As noted in Chapter 1, feminists persistently critique conceptual references in Western political theory. Epistemology has been one of these areas of rethinking by many feminists. Inspired by Hungarian theorist Georg Lukacs,[34] who argues the working classes' material positioning and conditions in social production shape their knowledge claims and insights, feminist standpoint theory argues for attention to the experiential knowledge available to women. With Lukacs, they argue that the oppressed have better knowledge of the world not because they are oppressed, but because of the very specific experiential and structural conditions from which the knowledge they produce emerges. These arguments reference "epistemology." Bringing epistemology into feminist theory means researching how we make knowledge claims about the world.

Nancy Hartsock's version of standpoint theory, developed in *Money, Sex and Power: Toward a Feminist Historical Materialism*,[35] takes as its point of departure the sexual division of labor in reproduction. While some men take care of children, most children are raised by women, as mothers, and in other relations such as sisters, aunts, grandmothers, or waged care workers. Collins shows how Black mothers work collectively, in community, in "reproductive" labor including carrying, giving birth to, and raising children. Feminists have always argued that there is nothing natural (even while there is infinite value) in women's role in child-rearing. It is historically constituted, not necessary or natural; caregiving is a role that has only become more obvious as a socially and politically constructed "choice" as technology and industrial production have made it more convenient for men to care in a direct and materially significant fashion for children. Standpoint feminists argue reproductive relationships and roles are naturalized, just as the two-class system of owners and workers appears natural to us as we engage in production. Exposure of, or seeing behind, the appearance of naturalized relations is necessary to establish a standpoint. A feminist standpoint is an accomplishment; it requires thought and reflection. We cannot simply see the social relations in what is naturalized; the knowledge is latent, waiting to be discovered as we critically reflect on differences between men's and women's developmental and material patterns of life.

Hartsock's work draws on Lukacs' Marxism, but also on Georg Hegel and feminist readings of Sigmund Freud on gender development, to establish that there exists a feminist standpoint. "Standpoint" is not the same as "perspective" or "point of view." Generically, as individuals, we have different points of view from which we see the world. For liberals, individuals abstracted from their material surroundings and activities develop legitimate knowledge by using their reason, working in groups, figuring out patterns of behavior, and establishing trends. Marxist theory, especially that of Lukacs, argues for the epistemic significance of laboring or not laboring on and with the natural world. For Lukacs, the proletariat not only will have irreconcilable interests from the owners of the means of production, but will, because of their common position in the division of labor and in relationship to the natural and machine world, have a more complete knowledge than the owning class of how the world works. Their knowledge will be qualitatively better, more holistic, and revolutionary as they will see/experience the necessities and ways of production and see/experience the dynamics of oppression from the bottom up.

Similarly, Hartsock argues a feminist standpoint emerges from the rich and varied terrain on which women contribute materially to the making of the common world. She takes Lukacs' argument about the standpoint of the proletariat and works it into the facts of the sexual division of labor structuring the reproduction *and*, importantly, the production of life. Women have never only worked in the home. Even as the expectation of "staying at home with the children" emerged with capitalism and industrial production, women worked outside the home, with much of their work reflecting "domestic" qualities. Black women worked in white households and the fields; white women worked in other households, in textile factories, and in service to male bosses; poor women worked every kind of service job. The "housewife" or, more recently, the "stay-at-home mom" has always been an ideal, not a reality for most women, even while women have typically been expected to be the primary caregivers to children and organizers of households. Hartsock argues that from the "home-work" that women do—whether in the formal economy or in the private space—emerges a standpoint, a knowledge that is more complete than that of men or male workers. Rather than discounting or diminishing the skills and difficulties involved in the material repetitive labor of cleaning and cooking and the social labor of raising boys and girls, Hartsock argues it produces a knowledge of the world superior to that of those who do not engage in such tasks.

Hartsock further draws on feminist psychological theories of child development—in particular, that of Nancy Chodorow[36]—to show that girls will have a more connected life because they need not separate from their primary caregiver (the mother) to become women. Boys must not only separate from the primary caregiver but must attempt to follow the path of the absent father, the abstract masculine figure. This puts boys, as they develop into masculine adults, in a defensive posture *vis-à-vis* femininity and a speculative and difficult posture *vis-à-vis* masculinity.

As pointed out when I discussed theories of the state of nature, Western political and social theory has been written from a masculinist standpoint, privileging competition, aggression, individualism, and death as primary attributes of social life. A feminist standpoint contests this dominant framing from the perspective of women's material and social situatedness. We can also look at the complex experience of pregnancy that (thus far) is available only to those identified as biologically female. Adrienne Rich wrote about motherhood as an institution and as an experience. Hartsock draws on Rich's description of pregnancy:

> In early pregnancy the stirring of the fetus felt like the ghostly tremors of my own body, later like the movement of a being imprisoned inside me; but both sensations were MY sensations, contributing to my sense of physical and psychic space.[37]

This extraordinary, unique (to pregnancy), and embodied experience of neither being together nor separate from the fetus offers a fundamentally different source of knowledge about social relations unrecognizable from the point of view offered by the masculinist canon of epistemological inquiry.

Patricia Hills Collins' study *Black Feminist Thought: Knowledge, Consciousness, and the Politics of Empowerment* shows how the historical experience of Black women in the US informs Black women's intellectual traditions. For Collins, Black women consistently ask what feminisms, as they emerge from very different experiences in the world, can make of and do with differences among us as we seek justice. Collins' sociological approach shows the difference that Black women's positioning as agricultural and domestic workers, in segregated rural and urban communities, and as mothers embedded in segregated Black communities makes to their perspectives about and within feminism. Collins emphasizes perspectives gained by way of daily life, not "over" abstract thought, but as a critical and primary aspect of Black feminists' contributions to academic inquiry and teaching. She thinks about power as oppressive, but also as circulating, as an intangible entity to which individuals stand in varying relationships in their daily lives as lived in relationship to different groups and institutions:

> Oppression is not simple understood in the mind—it is felt in the body in myriad ways . . . [Black woman's] gender may be more prominent when she becomes a mother, her race when she searches for housing, her social class when she applies for credit, her sexual orientation when she is walking with her lover, and her citizenship status when she applies for a job.[38]

Standpoint feminisms are about more than perspective. If "perspective" is the superficial angle of vision we reference, we can easily drift into liberal feminism. After all, common sense tells us that each individual has their own perspective and angle of vision when interpreting the world. This would mean that as we engage politically, we will argue from individualized perspectives and at best acknowledge that we all see the world differently as individuals and must come to some accommodation with one another. Standpoint feminisms root "perspective" in material circumstances and embodied labors which are differentiated by relationships of dominance and structural power. We are not disembodied individuals being abstractly "socialized" into perspectives and opinions. There are developmental and structural conditions, possibilities, and limitations on what and how we know and how we develop those perspectives and opinions. Standpoint feminists focus on sex differences and race/gendered differences in our material, psychological, and embodied lives. They argue forms of knowledge about the world that we take for granted or consider to be "settled truths" are gendered; they are produced through material, psychological, and embodied experience and relationships. If analyzed in historical context, they are partial, inadequate, and often dangerous to human life.

INTERSECTIONALITY AND FEMINISM

> Only the black woman can say "when and where I enter, in the quiet, undisputed dignity of my womanhood, without violence and without suing or special patronage, then and there the whole . . . race enters with me."
>
> Ann Julia Cooper[39]

Danielle Ponder, public defense attorney and musician from Buffalo, New York, called her recent album *Some of Us are Brave*. The reference is to an anthology titled *All the Women are White, All the Blacks are Men, but Some of Us are Brave*.[40] Ponder read the book in law school. In a recent interview, she said:

> Ain't no choice but to be brave. It's the fact that we exist in this intersection that makes us brave, the fact that we have to live in the world as both Black and as woman. If you do nothing else but wake up and breathe, holding those two identities and walking in this world is bravery.[41]

Her contemporary comment, her work as a public defender, and her lyrics as a musician reflect on decades of intersectional theorizing and study by feminist Black women.

The anthology Ponder references is credited as a founding moment of Black women's studies. In it, Black feminist thinkers critically engage with the Western canon of political thought and practice; liberalism and Marxism are sites of inspiration and critique. Further, "standpoint feminisms," an epistemological approach indebted to socialist theory, is referenced by Black feminists and informs insights offered by intersectional approaches to theorizing identity politics. The imperative to think in intersectional terms has changed research on and interpretations of experience and texts across academic disciplines and feminist organizing.

All the Women are White . . . and other writings by Black women and self-identified feminists over the last two centuries have constructed political arguments in the tradition of what we now commonly call "intersectionality." This term was coined by Kimberlé Crenshaw in 1989 as she wrote about how discrimination law fails to acknowledge the specificity of harms experienced by Black women; they could bring charges of discrimination as Black people or as women, but not as Black women.[42] Black women engage with law from a place that is experientially and structurally different from white women and Black men. While Crenshaw's initial use of the term referenced legal spaces and dynamics, work referencing intersectionality has carved significant conceptual pathways; it has become one of the most influential terms of art organizing theory and practice among feminists over the last 30 years. Patricia Hill Collins argues it has created a paradigm shift in feminism.[43]

Black women have always been active in public spaces, speaking out, resisting, and organizing. Black women theorize the particular experience of being a Black woman in the US, creating linkages to what in the 1970s were referred to as "Third-World radical women's struggles," and hold those who speak/write/act as feminists accountable for whether and how race, ethnicity, and class are integrated into theory and action in the name of women. As remarked in Chapter 1, "feminism" became commonly used as a term to describe certain kinds of theory and action related to white women in the early 20th century. Black women and women of color have countered this assumption in the academy and in politics with feminist theories about what it is to exist at the intersection of systems of oppression.

Black feminists address the material and structural conditions of Black women. The thinkers I reference here consistently critique liberalism (the assertion of or aspiration to race-blindness in the name of individual rights and equality), capitalism (the hyper-exploitation of people of color in social production and reproduction), and white supremacy (violence carried out in the name of sustaining the white race in its presumed superiority) simultaneously to develop analyses of oppression. What was named "intersectionality" by Crenshaw has emerged as an argument grounded in the idea that the historical facts of Black women's existence in the US are unique; Black women are subjected simultaneously to, and their identities have emerged in relationship to, systemic racial, class discrimination, and gender formations, none of which can be disentangled from the others in the lived experience of being Black and female—especially, in the US, that of chattel slavery and institutionalized exclusion by way of Jim Crow and segregationist policy.

The arguments associated with "intersectionality" have traveled under several different conceptual labels since the late 19th century. For all the complexities articulated below, "intersectionality" can be succinctly summarized—as in a recent interview Keeanga Yamahtta-Taylor recorded with Demita Frazier, co-author of the Combahee River Collective (CRC) Statement. Frazier tells the story of street harassment by a white man that included the terms "Black" and "pussy." She summarizes what the CRC Statement calls interlocking oppressions, now referred to as "intersectionality," when she says, ". . . and there is not a Black man [or a white woman] who will have that experience because Black and pussy, *you can't break that apart.*"[44]

The CRC was primarily a study group where women who were involved in reproductive justice and labor struggles came together to think and reflect on what they were doing. Frazier participated in writing their manifesto, titled the "Combahee River Collective Statement," which remains deeply influential among feminist theorists and activists. The CRC Statement argues for Black, gay women's unique positionality in understanding, confronting, and undoing oppression. The women wrote about their identities as socialist, lesbian, Black women. The statement says: "This focusing on our own oppression is embodied in the concept identity politics. We believe the most radical politics comes directly out of our own identity, as opposed to working to end someone else's oppression."[45] They claim it is essential to see identities as "interlocking": they do not "add up" as separate dynamics that make a whole person. It is the burdens and the possibilities of these identities that shape the collective's political action. It also draws together socialist (class), Black (racial), lesbian (sexuality), and feminist (gender and sex) perspectives. The statement explains that, as persons constructed as and through these identities, the actions they take are diverse, including but not limited to labor struggles, gay liberation, and anti-sterilization and anti-sexual violence work. Further, following from the experience and theory of interlocking oppressions, the statement explicitly addresses separatism in feminism, arguing that because they are Black, they experience racism alongside but differently from Black men. They must work as critical partners with, not apart from, Black men. "We struggle together with Black men against racism while we also struggle with Black men about sexism."[46]

These arguments about interlocking oppressions informed Crenshaw's thinking when she coined the term "intersectionality" in response to the failure of laws against discrimination to capture the particular harms against Black women, whose exclusion from opportunities in education and work exists in the gap in Title VII of race "and" sex. Crenshaw's work shows that Black women are unlocatable in policy, law, and cultural representations as both/and female and Black. She introduces her critique with the following insight:

> Although racism and sexism readily intersect in the lives of real people, they seldom do in feminist and antiracist practices. And so, when the practices expound identity as woman or person of

color as an either/or proposition, they relegate the identity of women of color to a location that resists telling.[47]

While in part about policy and legal gaps which effectively disappear the experiences of women of color, perpetuating discrimination and harm, Crenshaw's work recalls Audre Lorde's conceptualization of "difference" in an essay titled "Age, Race, Class and Sex: Women Redefining Difference."[48] Lorde argues for working with and against difference (not across or beyond) as it is lodged in ourselves in the shape of inequality, of subconscious assumptions of better and worse, dominant and subordinate. "Difference" has traditionally been defined in dualisms—male/female, white/Black, hetero/homosexuality, citizen/foreigner—with the first in each pairing constituting the norm, or the original, to which the second is compared. The normative side of the dualism identifies as superior and, in being the standard against which "others" are measured, it is dominant. Her oft-repeated assertion that "The master's tools will never dismantle the master's house" appears at the end of this essay, calling upon listeners (the essay was originally a public address at a conference) to experience "difference" differently. She is referring specifically to the way "differences" across race, sex, class, and age have been defined as valuing one race or sex or class or other identity as superior, and the "other" as less-than, in need of catching up with, becoming the same as, or imitating the superior identity. Revaluing difference means reaching inside the self to see where and how our reaction to difference lives. It means recognition of difference and equality *in* difference, not recognition only of that which potentially becomes the same or equality as conditioned by assimilation. Crenshaw's thinking is related to Lorde's as a way of responding to the question: what difference do the multiple differences among us make?" It is not, finally, about whether we avoid or embrace categorization writ large—about whether we have identities or are identified. It is about arguments as to the significance of identities as they emerge and change within the context of relationships of power and dominance; it studies how resources, material and cultural, are distributed as a result of passive or active identifications—in this case, of being a Black female.

Research that struggles with how to measure and assess phenomenon and experience at the intersections of systems of oppression and commentary on what intersectionality is has proliferated since the last decade of the 20th century. Patricia Hill Collins[49] argues that intersectionality can be thought about as a metaphor: consider the self as standing at an intersection at which forces and movement can come from multiple directions; or a hermeneutic, an assumed point of departure for research.

Just as radical feminist thinking entered mainstream institutional thinking about sexualized violence through Title IX discourse and claims about domestic violence, intersectionality has entered the mainstream lexicon through "diversity, equity, and inclusion" narratives and practices in workplaces and educational institutions. This has recently inspired critical thinking about whether, particularly in its popular and institutional uses, intersectionality as a reference to persons oppressed by multiple axes of oppression offers a convenient legitimating reference for the debunked (by anti-racist feminist thinkers) liberal discourse of "inclusivity" and "diversity." Does intersectionality on its own terms invite this kind of appropriation? Or is this a misappropriation of the insights it provides? These questions have driven what Jennifer Nash calls "the intersectionality wars."[50] Nash writes about how terms like "intersectionality" travel and change in meaning and significance in different contexts. She advocates that Black feminists not allow the appropriation by the mainstream or the predictable conservative backlash against criticisms produced by intersectional analysis to put them into a defensive crouch as to claims about the provenance or legitimacy of the concept. Instead, she argues that Black feminists should "let go" of intersectionality and think critically about how it travels through queer and transnational feminist theorizing.

QUEER THEORY

> Postmodern culture with its decentered subject can be the space where ties are severed, or it can provide the occasion for new and varied forms of bonding.
>
> bell hooks[51]

Queer theory and feminist theory are deeply and complexly entangled. Since its emergence in the 1980s, queer theory has been associated with deconstructive critiques of sex and sexuality. It is associated with "sex-positive" movements and thinkers who argue gender/sex binaries and the sexual essentialism associated with gendering human beings should be themselves historicized, not assumed. Feminist theory had been associated with gender identity and roles; with rethinking women's positioning in the world, but not with rethinking "women" as such. These associations are now quite blurred, though we continue to differentiate intuitively and in terms of the academic enterprise between queer theory and feminist theory.

In *Gender Trouble: Feminism and the Subversion of Identity*,[52] Judith Butler carries out the promise of the title as she de-naturalizes the male/female and feminine/masculine binaries and, consequently, normative heterosexuality. Challenging feminist theorizing that assumes a female/male body and a structured, gendered system into which those are slotted, Butler argues gender is performative; it is historically and philosophically shown to be detachable from biological sex and/or the heteronormative binaries that habituate us as to how and who we enact desire. The performative thesis influences feminists to argue that the subject is decentered—an effect, not an agent, of what Michel Foucault famously calls the "microphysics of power."[53] What Teresa de Lauretis later named as "queer theory"[54] argues subjects are akin to nodal points emerging in contingent and sometimes accidental ways at the intersections of complex webs of power relationships. Once a derogatory insult against those who are or are perceived to be gay, the word "queer" was claimed as part of the gay pride movement in the late 1980s. Since then, "queering" has come to be used as a verb meaning, in the most general sense, "to render the familiar strange." One can argue that feminism is always rendering the familiar (women as natural caregivers, sex objects, carriers of moral tradition, emotional/irrational) strange by way of historical recovery, radical activism, and critique of gender norms. However, there is an element in feminism, challenged by queer theory, that seeks out what it would be to be a "woman" or women outside of power relations. Standpoint theory, for example, ultimately argues that there is more truth (not "the" truth) in subjugated knowledges and better insights driven by the (re)productive work of those subject to dominance.

While queer theory seems like a contradiction of feminist aspirations, *if* feminism requires centering women's subject status and agency as prior to politics, there are, nonetheless, points of connection. Donna Haraway, a feminist thinker who draws on socialist and postmodern thinking, once remarked on a question she was asked at a conference: "Do you (Haraway) believe in reality?" Her response turned on the term "believe." She remarked: "If one 'believes' in reality, is it real or something else?"[55] This response is a queering style of inquiry; rather than answering a question, she asks about the construction of the question. However, in 1991, Haraway wrote: ". . . my problem and 'our' problem is how to have simultaneously an account of radical historical contingency for all knowledge claims and knowing subjects . . . and a no-nonsense commitment to faithful accounts of a 'real' world . . ."[56] Queer theory insists on the irreducible differences among and consequent radical multiplicity of knowledges that jostle and contest for position and legitimacy in the public space. Like socialist and some standpoint theory, feminists engaged with queer theory argue that the problem with masculinist forms of knowledge and politics is the insistence on "objective" (disembodied and detached from material/social contingencies) knowledge. Queer feminisms insist not on "true" or "essential" identities like "woman" (as the WI-W manifesto claims) and/or even interlocking identities, which assume already established subject formations (as the CRC Statement suggests); their focus is on the coming into being of contingent identities as effects of forcefields of knowledge and power. Hence, bell hooks' comment on the possibilities of decentering the subject as allowing for new possibilities of connection, albeit temporary.

Ultimately, our knowledge of the world is partial. This is not a new insight. However, as Haraway asserts: "The standpoints of the subjugated are not 'innocent' (objective or free from power) positions. *On the contrary, they are preferred because in principle they are least likely to allow denial of the critical and interpretive core of all knowledge.*"[57] Feminism must acknowledge its enmeshment in power and reflect on its potential to become another regulatory/disciplinary apparatus. We may prefer that regulatory/disciplinary apparatus, but we should not assume in advance it will be clean or innocent of power or even relationships of dominance. Another way of thinking about what Haraway says here is to note that feminists, as exemplified by the self-criticism of the Miss America protest in 1968, consistently consider how feminisms may be reproducing the systems they are trying to undo in the name of justice. For example, in criticizing the women who competed in the Miss America pageant, when it was the system that constitutes sexual objectification as the most lucrative path for women to take, they were potentially colluding with conservatives who moralize about women who sell their sexuality to make a living. As I discuss in Chapter 4, feminists persistently challenge thinking about what it means to sell or objectify sex. In this view, consistent attention to the nexus of power and knowledge keeps feminism attentive to its enmeshment in relations of power.

That knowledge and politics are essentially critical and interpretive "all the way down" is the point of departure for feminists who take up queer theory. They critique efforts of radical and socialist feminists to assert any essential commonality among women across time and space on experiential or material grounds. The radicalism of queered feminism lies in its challenge to any feminist demands for commonality "under the skin," whether those ideally exist beyond class differences or beyond race. To seek an authentic "womanness" takes feminism as such outside of history and thus renders it as apart from politics. Butler, for example, shows how, historically, every time a group asserts an "identity," there are dissenters, critics, self-identified outliers who contest the identity. The contemporary reference to the LGBTQIA+ community is an example. It shows the persistent emergence and contestation of sexed/gendered identities. The "+" sign indicates the infinite potential for sex/gendered identity formations to emerge and suggests identities not only proliferate, but do not stay in place. As importantly, they emerge in relationship to other identity formations, as contestations. How can feminism do its work considering this persistent contestation when the world is riven with consistent forms of oppression and violence against persons identified as women and other historically and materially subjugated figures according to the groups with which they are, voluntarily or involuntarily, identified?

Rather than essential to the self, queer theory argues that identities—such as man, woman, lesbian, Black woman, Third World, transgender—are signifiers held in place by norms that demand repetition and performance. They are held in place by discipline (which includes incentives and disincentives) and harmfully punitive reactions. If we do not perform those identities "properly," we may be punished, excluded, or disdained by the dominant class;

but also, importantly, by those we claim solidarity with—as in persons who are not "Black enough," or femme and butch lesbians accused of imitating heterosexual norms of masculinity and femininity. In other words, identity is regulatory. This does not make it wrong or bad. Butler is not making moral judgments here; rather, she is making a political argument that "identity categories tend to be instruments of regulatory regimes, whether as the normalizing categories of oppressive structures or as the rallying points for a liberatory contestation of that very oppression."[58]

What does it mean, then, to say that gender and, by implication, other identities are performative, not essential to who we are and what we are capable of? Does the "performativity thesis" suggest that we can take our genders and sexualities on and off at will, enacting what "feels right" at any given moment? Is gender like a stage play? The response to this invites reference to psychic sensibilities about what feels real to us as we live in our everyday identities, what kinds of changes of consciousness we experience as we move from place to place—like Collins' representation of Black women as they move in and out of different communities and institutionalized spaces, and the very real pleasures and dangers of challenging regulatory norms. If women as "mothers" withdraw their labor, a "threat" implicit in arguments for reproductive justice, they and those who help them (e.g., medical professionals) face criminal sanctions. We are seeing this play out globally in response to struggles to establish bodily autonomy and reproductive justice for those identified as women. When women challenge the "naturalness" of their positioning as breeders, criminal sanctions often become more intense.

Another way to think about this: when we define "female," is there a way to know what that is without reference to the male? Is there a way to understand homosexuality without reference to heterosexuality? Can we know race without acknowledging the normative place held by whiteness? These are known as "dualisms." One side cannot exist without reference to the other. However, one side persistently asserts itself as the original and hence normative (qualitatively settled in status) such that—back to Aristotle—the female body was to be the inversion of the normative male body and the woman, therefore, the inferior, or second, sex. Heterosexuality, whether with reference to the Bible or more generally to "nature," asserts itself as the original, with homosexuality as derivative and again as secondary. It is the myth of being the original that sustains whiteness, maleness, heterosexuality as the norms against which "others" are measured and always found lacking.

To say gender is performative is not to say we can take it on or off at will. A better question is: what happens when we *do* resist through enacting identity outside the norm? What happens when claims are made about the fluidity, contingency, historicity of identity? Psychic, cultural, and material consequences follow, and new regulatory regimes emerge. There is no foreseeable or predictable "liberated" future in store if we (finally) find the singular cause of systemic oppression.

Queer theory challenges feminism to rethink its commitments to "identity." Radical feminists, for example, are committed to discovering the identity of "women," presumed to already be there for the finding. The radical hope is that an essential "womanness" will be found as women come together and share experiences. The CRC Statement asserts: "We believe that the most profound and radical politics come directly out of our own identity, as opposed to working to end someone else's oppression."[59] Socialist feminists argue our true identity is prior to politics as it is linked to our everyday material activity. Each of these examples presupposes "identities" that are there outside, or prior to, relationships of power. The identities described—whether monist (woman) or multiple (intersectional)—will be found if we strip away patriarchal, white supremacist, and ruling class ideologies and practices. This requires struggle and engagement but also ascribes an innocence (of power) to these subjugated identity formations. It suggests an authentic subject will be discovered or found (not created) through struggle and enlightenment.

Queer theory, emergent in relationship to feminist and poststructuralist theory, questions commitments to establishing the "roots" or the "origins" of social phenomenon or identities. This supplements Audre Lorde's argument that "difference" need not be about dominance. To be the original is to be the measure against all else is understood. To establish an "original" (the male/female binary from which gender norms are derived), with the "male" being asserted as the original against which the female is defined and measured, is to sustain a static site of normalcy.

This results in debates, for example, about whether women must "learn" to live in a man's world to "make it" or whether, for example, enlistment in the military by women is a concession to an "essentially" masculinist institution in the name of formal equality. Eventually, we ask whether they reproduce the "origin" story: men created it, so women must measure up, take down the institution, or refuse. They do not get to create. However, this debate begs the question as to whether the military and other masculinist institutions change with the entry of women. What happens as these institutions become "feminized" or made to "include" different kinds of bodies, identities, and sexualities?

This suggests that dominant categories or identities are more fragile than some feminist thinking has asserted. Heterosexuality and masculinity are no more "real" or original than queerness. It is repetition, structures of power and naturalized dominance, and often brute force that keep them in place. Arguments among feminists with respect to queer theory are over the assertion of identity as necessary to "successful" political movements against dominant classes and structures of power. Leaving liberal feminism aside for the moment (though most liberal feminists also argue for collective action "as women" in terms of changing public policy), feminists of all kinds have argued the grounds for collective struggle must be discovered prior to the enactment of politics. Consciousness-raising was founded on the practice coming to shared consciousness/identity *and then* entering politics. Feminist theory has not come to any consensus about queering its own terms of legitimacy—that grounded in a common identity prior to political engagement and/or material activity that is in its origins social and economic, and only when critiqued and challenged "political." Queer theorizing and activism asks whether feminism can claim outsider status to the power relationships it critiques. This discussion continues in the next chapter as I review contemporary texts that attempt to define "feminism" and express views about what it means to "be" a feminist and/or live "as" a feminist.

TRANSNATIONAL FEMINISMS

In Chapter 1, I referred to a speech given by Sojourner Truth, a Black female activist who became notorious on the abolitionist speaker circuit of the antebellum era in the US for speaking her mind with or without permission from the typically white organizers of public meetings. I discussed her challenge to the identity of "woman." Here I discuss the significance of the distortion of her words by a suffragist activist.

Gage's version imposes a southern "slave" dialect, whereas Truth's first language was Dutch. Truth was raised in New York and did not speak with a southern dialect. The intent in revising the content and dialect of her speech was to make Truth appeared *more* like an oppressed, escaped, female slave inspiring northern abolitionists to have more sympathy with an oppressed and submissive subject.

This is one example of what feminist theorists have grappled with in terms of the dynamics of "speaking for" others who are oppressed. It is one example of what Gayatri Spivak asked in the title of her historic challenge to Western intellectuals' thinking about "third-world subjects" in the era of anti-colonial independence struggles: "Can the Subaltern Speak?"[60]

Antonio Gramsci, an Italian Marxist writing in the early 20th century, used "subaltern" as a descriptive term to describe the systemically oppressed. He offers a framework for understanding how systemic oppression works, using the term "hegemony" to describe how capitalism operates as a system in which the line between coercion and consent is consistently being redrawn in favor of ruling classes. Sometimes more force is necessary to sustain dominance; other times, the underclasses, or the subaltern classes, are persuaded or consent to the conditions of their oppression, without seeing or knowing it as such.[61] Of course, Spivak knows those categorized as "subaltern" or subjugated can speak in the literal sense. Sojourner Truth spoke a *lot*. The meaning of what they say, however, is hijacked by dominant, normative conceptualizations of who they are and of their actions.

Spivak tells another story of a historical woman who went to great lengths to make sure the truth of her actions would be represented in a world in which she knew her femaleness/femininity would otherwise "explain" her every action. As a revolutionary in a war of independence, she is asked to carry out an assassination as she enters the struggle. She cannot bring herself to carry out the assassination. Rather than sacrifice the trust of the revolutionary comrades, she hangs herself. She waits, however, until she is menstruating to make sure that the meaning of her action would not be interpreted as a response to an illicit pregnancy. Nonetheless, her action is interpreted after her death, by her own comrades, as a caricatured feminine response to failed love. She could not "speak" if the point of speaking is to be understood as one intends. She is rendered by her comrades as a tragic feminine figure, eliding the significance of the public/political choices she was being asked to make.

Spivak's critique is directed at Western intellectuals' representations of the oppressed subjects of the "third world." Spivak shows how Western epistemology, stemming from Marxism, says the oppressed either know and are spoken for by vanguard intellects or know and speak for themselves in an authentic and essential manner. This limited construction of knowledge production and representation means the subaltern cannot "speak."

Spivak's question about representation resonates with an earlier critique articulated by Chandra Mohanty of a tendency in Western feminist thinking to homogenize the "Third-World Woman" as an objectively oppressed figure who exists outside of history.[62] Mohanty criticizes some Western feminist approaches to the increasingly global reach of feminism, arguing they reproduce Western-centric constructions of the "traditional other" of underdeveloped social systems. This critique has much in common with radical constructionist arguments that the meaning of material and social practices constitutes subjects. Those identified as women *become* wives, daughters, mothers, workers, in certain sets of social conditions.

It is the diverse and often contradictory meanings of material practices the theorist should work with, not the potential for finding (and then, by implication, helping) a universal subject that is the oppressed woman. For example, Western liberalism constructs child marriage as something primitive black and brown men do to black and brown girls and women, thus erasing the multiple meanings and interpretations of these practices as they happen in different contexts and different material circumstances. Simply invoking the phrase "child marriage" evokes an activity and subjectivity that are "other" to the modern West and presumably singular in their meaning to those practicing and/or being forced into it. For Mohanty, asserting that some form of authentic woman-ness exists behind, before, or beyond the practice that constitutes subjects as "child brides" is the wrong approach. Further, Western feminists should not assume—particularly after the trenchant critiques they themselves have issued—that "individual choice" describes what women in so-called liberal democracies are doing when they marry.[63]

Transnational feminisms have emerged with these critiques of Western hegemonic forms of knowledge production about "others" of the "non-Western world." We can see from the story about Sojourner Truth's speech that efforts to capture differences among women across axes of structural privilege to theorize conditions and propose potentially liberatory pathways often lead to misrepresentation, reproducing the very structures of privilege feminists think they are challenging.

With insights from Black feminists committed to intersectional thought and practice, transnational feminisms engage critically with postmodern theories that decenter the subject as one who speaks in an authentic voice or is spoken for by intellectuals. Transnational feminist theory argues that the "other," constructed through what Edward Said called the Orientalizing project of Western knowledges,[64] is a projection required for the self-standing and stability of the European or Western subject to exist at all. The West cannot be, as such, without its other.

Transnational feminisms join those arguing for intersectional analysis in critiquing feminisms that reproduce binary categories at any level—of gender, global/local, center/periphery, First/Third worlds, white/Black, or developed/underdeveloped.

Like feminists who engage with race and queer theory, transnational feminist scholarship undoes feminist assumptions about woman as a category of being with underlying commonalities. It also, importantly, shows how gender identity—particularly that of the binary man/woman—maps onto nationalist discourses. This is not particular to nationalist struggles of the 20th century. It traces to the very emergence of the nation-state system and its spread across the last five centuries. Transnational feminists, as the name implies, critique the "nation" as it is sustained by gendered norms and expectations that differ across time and space.

Another thread woven through this scholarship references whether feminisms should be more concerned with identity or structure. This is not a question unique to transnationalist inquiry, but observing and interpreting women's agency at the local level is argued here to require a comparative spirit which means the deep consideration of relative positionality within structures of dominance and power. Individualizing or particularizing experience will not help us to understand the structures that constitute and make the form of experience possible in the first place.

The editors of *Scattered Hegemonies*[65] describe transnational feminism as a critique of the discursive tendencies of global feminism to repeat the dualisms of Western theorizing. Transnational feminisms would, the editors argue, cut across the lines of the center/periphery axis, pluralizing and deconstructing those assumed structures of dominance. This they had in common with feminists working on intersectionality to show it is necessary, not optional (or a decision a researcher should make for "analytical purposes"), to challenge the idea that anyone is ever just a man or a woman, always dominant or subordinate, or always the same in terms of unequal status, in social and political and cultural relationships. The essays in *Scattered Hegemonies* address representations of women's agency in historical and fictional settings. The editors say: "We need to articulate the relationship of gender to scattered hegemonies such as global economic structures, patriarchal nationalisms, 'authentic' forms of tradition, local structures of domination, and legal-juridical oppression on multiple levels."[66]

This argues for a feminism that remains focused on gender but always in the context of the dynamics otherwise named, never thinking gender as such exists outside of them as we theorize. Transnationalist thinkers bring gender into focus as a dynamic process, arguing that we are engendered in complex conditions not of our own making and not in relationship to a singular dominant force. They thus show how women and men participate in complex ways that may reproduce or resist or concede or revolutionize. A concrete example is the work of a coalition that called itself Women Living Under Muslim Laws.[67] This group collected dossiers of individual women living under, resisting, and engaging with the many varied forms of law identified with Islam. The dossiers are used by the organization for various purposes, including to argue refugee status. However, they also show that there is no singular "Muslim law," or "oppressed Muslim woman." This challenges Muslim fundamentalists who wish to assert one law they can identify as Islam and Western theory and policy that represents Muslim men as tyrannical and Muslim women as hapless victims, thereby justifying the ongoing violence by both fundamentalists and the liberal West against regimes and peoples identified with Islam.

CONCLUSION

This chapter summarizes and reviews significant texts and conceptual developments in feminist theory as they relate to and challenge traditions in Western political thought. We have explored the critiques and the possibilities offered by feminist thinkers and activists since the 1960s. Arguments about what women have in common and those about how differences among those who self-identify as women should shape feminism framed this discussion of feminist theorizing. Reflection on what we mean when referencing "woman," "gender," "intersectionality," and "difference" frustrates, inspires, and motivates scholars and activists, and continues to generate questions about how to understand history, the present, and efforts to move into a better future.

Feminist theory has never only been about women or gender. It contributes to understanding and critiquing the general complexities of the world(s) we live in together. The following chapters take up the question of what renders an analysis "feminist" and whether it is important to sustain that term as a descriptor. I will discuss when and why it has become so fraught as a reference point, among the general public, among those who identify as women, and among self-identified feminists themselves.

NOTES

1 King, Deborah, "Multiple Jeopardy, Multiple Consciousness: The Context of Black Feminist Ideology" in *Signs* vol. 14 1 (1988) 42–72.

2 MacKinnon, Catharine, *Feminism Unmodified* (Harvard University Press, 1988).

3 Donovan, Josephine, *Feminist Theory: The Intellectual Traditions* (Continuum Press, 2012).

4 Tong, Rosemarie, *Feminist Thought: A More Comprehensive Introduction* (Routledge, 2024).

5 Eisenstein, Zillah, *The Radical Future of Liberal Feminism* (Longman Press, 1981).

6 Jaggar, Allison, *Feminist Politics and Human Nature* (Roman and Littlefield, 1983).

7 Nussbaum, Martha, *Women and Human Development* (Cambridge University Press, 2000).

8 Brennan, Teresa and Carol Patemen, "Mere Auxiliaries to the Commonwealth: Women and the Origins of Liberalism" in *Political Studies* vol. 27 2 (1979) 183–200.

9 Locke, John, *The Second Treatise on Government* (Hackett Press, 1980).

10 Okin, Susan Muller, *Justice, Gender, and the Family* (Basic Books, 1991).

11 For a brief description, see Nussbaum, Martha, "Human Rights and Human Capabilities" in *Harvard Human Rights Journal* vol. 20 (2007). https://journals.law.harvard.edu/hrj/wp-content/uploads/sites/83/2020/06/20HHRJ21-Nussbaum.pdf

12 Okin, ibid. 140.

13 Ferguson, Micheale, "Vulnerability by Marriage: Okin's Radical Feminist Critique of Structural Gender Inequality" in *Hypatia* vol. 31 3 (2016) 687–703.

14 Spruill, Marjorie, *Divided We Stand: The Battle over Women's Rights and Family Values that Divided America* (Bloomsbury, 2017).

15 Echols, Alice, *Daring to be Bad: Radical Feminism in America 1967–1975* (University of Minnesota Press, 1984).

16 Koedt, Ann, "The Myth of the Vaginal Orgasm" in Anne Koedt (ed.) *Radical Feminism* (Quadrangle Books, 1973).

17 Firestone, Shulamith, *The Dialectic of Sex: The Case for Feminist Revolution* (Bantam Books, 1970).

18 MacKinnon, Catharine, *Feminism Unmodified* (Harvard University Press, 1988).

19 Firestone, ibid. 4

20 Firestone, ibid. 12

21 MacKinnon, ibid. 48

22 MacKinnon, Catharine, "Feminism, Marxism, Method and the State" in *Signs* vol. 7 3 (1988) 515.

23 MacKinnon, Catharine, *The Sexual Harassment of Working Women* (Yale University Press, 1979).

24 De Beauvoir, Simone, *The Second Sex* (Vintage, 1989). This text cannot be "assigned" within the framing of this chapter. It is canonical in the sense that it has deeply influenced women's theorizing and activism and is required reading (at least parts of it) in feminist theory classes.

25 Radicalesbians, "Woman-Identified-Women," in Anne Koedt (ed.) *Radical Feminism* (Quadrangle Press, 1973) 240–245.

26 Ibid. 240.

27 Wittig, Monique, *The Straight Mind* (Beacon Press, 1992).

28 Radicalesbians, ibid.

29 Marx, Karl "The Eighteenth Brumaire of Louis Bonaparte" in Robert C. Tucker (ed.) *The Marx-Engels Reader* (W.W. Norton and Company, 1978) 595.

30 Ferguson, Ann, *Sexual Democracy: Women, Oppression and Revolution* (Routledge Press, 1991) 44.

31 Davis, Angela, *Women, Race and Class* (Vintage Press, 1983).

32 Jaggar, Allison, *Feminist Politics and Human Nature* (Rowman and Allenheld/Harvester Press, 1983).

33 Federici, Sylvia, "Theses on Wages for Housework" (1974), cited in Federici, Sylvia and Jill Richards, "Every Woman is a Working Woman," *Boston Review*, December 19, 2018. https://www.bostonreview.net/articles/every-woman-working-woman/

34 Lukacs, Georg *History and Class Consciousness* (MIT Press, 1972).

35 Hartsock, Nancy, *Money, Sex and Power: Toward a Feminist Historical Materialism* (Northeastern University Press, 1985).

36 Chodorow, Nancy, *The Reproduction of Mothering: Psychoanalysis of the Sociology of Gender* (University of California Press, 1978).

37 Rich, Adrienne, *Of Woman Born: Motherhood as Experience and Institution* (Norton Press, 1995).

38 Collins, Patricia Hill, *Black Feminist Thought: Knowledge, Consciousness, and the Politics of Empowerment* (Routledge Press, 2008) 274–275.

39 Cooper, Julia Anne, cited in Giddings, Paula, *When and Where I Enter* (William Morrow, 1996).

40 Hull, Gloria, Patricia Hill-Scott and Barbara Smith, *All the Women are White, All the Blacks are Men, but Some of Us are Brave* (Feminist Press, 1982).

41 Kushner, Daniel, "Danielle Ponder—a Singer Who Was Once a Lawyer—Enjoys Critical Raves," National Public Radio, September 17, 2022. https://www.npr.org/2022/09/17/1123657145/danielle-ponder-a-singer-who-was-once-a-lawyer-enjoys-critical-raves

42 Crenshaw, Kimberlé, "Mapping the Margins: Intersectionality, Identity Politics, and Violence Against Women of Color" in *Stanford Law Review* vol. 43 6 (1991) 1241–1299.

43 Collins, Patricia Hill, *Intersectionality as Critical Social Theory* (Duke University Press, 2019).

44 Yahmahtta-Taylor, Keeyanga, "A Conversation with Demita Frazier" Social Justice Initiative, February 20, 2024. https://sji.uic.edu/events/demita-frazier/

45 The Combahee River Collective, "A Black Feminist Statement" reprinted in *Women's Studies Quarterly* vol. 24 3 (2014) 271–280.

46 Combahee, ibid.

47 Crenshaw, ibid. 1242

48 Lorde, Audre, "Age, Race, Class and Sex: Women Redefining Difference" in *Sister Outsider* (Crossing Press, 1984).

49 Collins, Patricia Hill, ibid.

50 Nash, Jennifer "Rethinking Intersectionality" in *Feminist Review* vol. 89 1 (2008) 1–15.

51 hooks, bell, "Postmodern Blackness," University of Pennsylvania African Studies Center, April 19, 1994. https://www.africa.upenn.edu/Articles_Gen/Postmodern_Blackness_18270.html

52 Butler, Judith, *Gender Trouble* (Routledge Press, 1990).

53 Foucault, Michel, *Discipline and Punish.* Alan Sheridan trans. (Vintage Books, 1995) 170.

54 De Lauretis, Teresa, "Queer Theory: Origins of Queer Theory." https://science.jrank.org/pages/10938/Queer-Theory-Origins-Queer-Theory.html

55 "A Giant Bumptious Litter: Donna Haraway on Truth, Technology, and Resisting Extinction," *Logic(s)* Issue 9, December 7, 2019. https://logicmag.io/nature/a-giant-bumptious-litter/

56 Haraway, Donna, "Situated Knowledges: The Science Question in Feminism and the Privilege of Partial Perspective" in *Feminist Studies* vol. 14 3 (1988) 579.

57 Ibid. 584.

58 Butler, Judith, "Imitation and Gender Insubordination" in Henry Abelove et al. (eds.) *The Lesbian and Gay Studies Reader* (Routledge, 1993) 308.

59 "The Combahee River Collective Statement," written by the CRC as a collaborative project, was first published in Eisenstein, Zillah, *Capitalist Patriarchy and the Case for Socialist-Feminism* (NYU Press, 1979) 362–372.

60 Spivak, Gayatri "Can the Subaltern Speak?" in Cary Nelson and Lawrence Grossman (eds) *Marxism and the Interpretation of Culture* (Macmillan, 1988) 271–318.

61 Gramsci, Antonio, *The Prison Notebooks* (International Publishers Press, 1971).

62 Mohanty, Chandra, "Under Western Eyes: Feminist Scholarship and Colonial Discourses" in *Boundary 2* vol. 12 3 (1984) 333–358.

63 Ibid.

64 Said, Edward, *Orientalism* (Vintage Books, 1979).

65 Grewal, Inderpal and Caren Kaplan (eds.) *Scattered Hegemonies* (University of Minnesota Press, 1994).

66 Ibid. 17

67 See https://www.wluml.org/ for information about the organization Women Living Under Muslim Law.

3

FEMINISMS AND POLICY IN THE 20TH AND 21ST CENTURIES

INTRODUCTION

As discussed in Chapter 1, willingness to identify as feminist has ebbed and flowed over the century during which the term has been used to describe thinking and policy about women and gender. Feminisms ask questions that inspire policy proposals that address intersectional, structural oppression. Thinking like feminists keeps us thinking and acting critically about the world but also about our own assumptions and plans. This book argues that, no matter its public reputation, feminist analysis is necessary as it digs deeper and critically reflects on why strategies like enforcing anti-discrimination statutes, making abortion legal, criminalizing domestic violence, and getting more women into positions of power have not yet made the kinds of differences in women's lives that advocates wish to see, have had such uneven success rates, or have perpetuated or created other social injustices. Feminist analysis also allows us to bear witness to success and engage, always with a critical edge, with how the world is changing in accordance with what feminists have been arguing and acting on for decades.

As we have seen, feminists bring diverse lenses to the study of and engagement with politics. Feminists, through argument and action, expose and challenge deeply entrenched assumptions about justice, progress, equality, rights, power, and other normative concepts. These are concepts we tend to reference as if we already know and agree on what we are talking about. Feminist analyses of

DOI: 10.4324/9781003264682-3

issues framed by these concepts are deeply controversial because they ask questions (as we will see in the discussion of Sara Ahmed's book)[1] invisible to or deliberately occluded by the customs, habits of thought, and behaviors of those with influence, power, or positions of dominance.

In this chapter, I discuss political issues and public policy. "Political" issues affect the public, are discussed in the public space, and generate conflictual interpretations and solutions. They impact everyone represented by a government, whether they are immediately aware of it or not. "Public policy" is defined as what governments do on behalf of or in service to the public. Keep in mind that units of government are not limited to nation-states; the United Nations, with its global reach, is also a governing apparatus. The issue areas addressed in this chapter each also involve legal or regulatory action that polices and shapes the actions/behaviors of all persons and groups in the many kinds of political communities in which they live or with which they identify (municipalities, provinces, states, nations, global). This chapter discusses a selection of issues that are particularly controversial among feminists researching, taking actions, and speaking out, in history and in the contemporary moment.

Mary Hawkesworth[2] argues feminists develop research approaches and policy ideas that are neither gender biased nor gender neutral. In other words, feminist research and ideas will ultimately serve women's and men's interests; we do not assume that gendered differences should not matter in the construction of policy. As Hawkesworth argues, feminists show that no issues are gender neutral and all policy impacts people as gendered subjects differently in systematic and empirically evident ways. In countries with gender-neutral family leave policies for men and women, for example, women leave the workforce in greater numbers to be primary caregivers. While some researchers argue women are violent against men in roughly equal numbers, the kind of violence men use against women (closed fists rather than slaps, guns rather than household objects) is more injurious and deadly, while women's violence is typically defensive. Research has shown that journalism has improved in treating men and women similarly in local coverage, neutralizing gendering effects[3]; but men and women continue to be judged by the public in spaces beyond mainstream journalism on fundamentally different grounds as to how they rule or represent their constituents in political office. For example, women's status as mothers is discussed while they campaign or are in office, while men's status as fathers is rarely mentioned. In other words, feminists show how gender differences and inequality are baked into political discussions and apparently gender-neutral policies. Policy thus requires ongoing feminist critique, analysis, and proposals that consider how gendered differences matter and whether we are approaching gender justice in implementing them.

Feminists across the globe take very different approaches to gender justice work; we work as outsiders or insiders to state and international institutions and influence sometimes incremental and sometimes sweeping changes in policy. Whether policies fought for by feminists, as insiders or outsiders to mainstream institutions, are successful is a complex question. Some benefit mostly women already privileged by other identity markers, as did affirmative action. Others are paternalistic and controlling, as are the welfare and development policies of the World Bank. As we will see in a later section, efforts to combat violence against women and girls and boys have served to legitimate the flawed criminal legal system and failed to prevent or offer justice for egregious sexualized harms. However, feminists never cease to think about and critique what is done in the name of feminism. It turns out feminists are our own best critics when assessing "success." My intent here is to show the reader how the multiple and critical perspectives feminisms bring to these issues open up diverse possibilities for political engagement and policy solutions. There is no one feminist approach to policy analysis and policymaking.

When discussing policy, it is also important to note that historical socioeconomic and cultural changes impact gender relationships and policy changes. Globally, since the 1970s, more people who identify as women are in the formal workforce. This requires a shift in caregiving of children. Though women still do the bulk of that work in heterosexual households, increasing numbers of people who identify as men express desire to be involved with their children beyond being a "breadwinner." These trends render it more likely that women will, still with difficulty, make independent livings and be in a material position to make choices beyond what male figures in their families or communities implicitly or explicitly demand. However, these socioeconomic shifts are determined in large part by the demands of capitalism that make it necessary for all individuals of majority age and often younger in middle-class or poor families to work, and for single and/or poor women to engage in low-waged hourly labor while raising young children. Non-feminist analyses would not capture the additional burdens economic shifts place on women because, while numbers in the workplace may be equal, little else about the 24/7 essential tasks of domestic (e.g., the home) and civic (e.g., schools) reproduction is equally distributed.

Feminists look at complex global conditions in which climate change has vastly disparate impacts on women and men; in which more women are in the formal workforce than ever before, reporting of sexual violence is increasing, and women are entering institutions of higher education in higher numbers than men; and continue to ask questions about whether, because of these trends, women are achieving autonomy and liberty as gendered subjects. They further ask: are women in government or in the workplace reproducing the unjust legal, capitalist, and racial formations that render this "progress" possible for white women of a certain background while continuing to exclude, implicitly and explicitly, women of color and poor women? Does increased reporting of sexual violence—which typically means working with and trying to reform the established criminal legal system—serve the carceral state apparatus more so than women's progress toward independence and wellbeing?

Feminists expose and interpret the impacts and influence of male-dominated forms of rule by looking at the broader context of specific policy responses. We analyze by way of theory and empirical analysis how these forms morph into new guises in the contemporary era when even mainstream feminist analyses and solutions are familiar yet still demonized by some, considered "divisive" by others, and generally marginalized.

FEMINISTS AND CLIMATE POLICY—HUMAN/NATURE RELATIONSHIPS AND CLIMATE JUSTICE

There is a deep connection between feminisms and environmental politics and policy: numerous empirical studies show women, because they are more likely to work in subsistence modes of production and caring for others, suffer the effects of environmental degradation and climate change more than men. As heads of households and community leaders in marginalized communities, women have taken the lead in many local, national, and international campaigns to prevent and respond to environmental disasters.

Feminisms argue gender dynamics are intertwined with how nature and the climate are understood and treated by human beings. Dominant modernist ideas and practices like liberalism and Marxism understand "nature" as a resource, a means to other ends (human flourishing), and a site of competition for power and influence. For example, the domination of nature is considered key to self-(human) preservation and undergirds the argument for accumulation central to liberalism and its attendant economic system, capitalism. It is also central to the vision of freedom defined in Marxism as the capacity to labor, to transform nature into products useful to humans, and thereby to live on terms that transcend necessity, which is identified with biological imperatives and hence the "natural." Both liberalism and Marxism argue that the perpetual transformation of nature from one thing to another (what is called economic growth and/or development), by way of human labor and extraction, is not only inherent in the human/nature relationship but necessary to human flourishing. Feminisms challenge these embedded assumptions about the human/nature relationship—assumptions which result in practices that fundamentally change conditions on earth necessary for human survival. Feminists offer critical resources for thinking about environmental and climate policy that move us beyond the current sense of crisis and into a sustainable and just future.

In this section, I discuss the work against environmental degradation and climate change being done by transnational feminists. Through the auspices of the United Nations and because of the vast network of feminist-inspired and adjacent organizations working in the area, the influence of women, the differential gendered impact of environmental degradation, and feminist-inspired solutions are commonly studied, if not fully accepted in practice.

One thread of feminist analysis and activism, known as "ecofeminism," has been particularly influential in challenging mainstream ideas about environmental and climate policy. In the early 1970s, as activism and policymaking specific to environmental degradation and sustainability emerged as a visible force in national and international politics, some feminists were developing gynocentric, spiritual, and material critiques of capitalist and colonialist exploitation and abuse of the resources offered to humans by the Earth and its ecological bounty. In 1973, Francoise d'Eaubonne coined the term "ecofeminism" to describe these approaches. As for many ideas and practices of feminism, interest in ecofeminism has ebbed and flowed over the decades. In the early decades of the environmental movements, ecofeminist thinkers and activists were so influential as to have their ideas and propositions integrated in the Rio Earth Summit of 1992 hosted by the United Nations. By the time of the Rio+20 summit in 2012, the healing and materialist discourses of the ecofeminists had been displaced in mainstream, official meetings by the fix-it discourses of managerial and market-oriented capitalism.[4] Since 2010, however, various ideas and practices of ecofeminism have also sustained increasing critical attention from and discussion by grassroots activists and feminists.

Ecofeminism emerged as a challenge to global capitalist and colonialist imperatives that nature is there to be mastered to improve the human condition. The initial connection between ecological and environmental concerns and feminism was drawn by way of showing how patriarchal culture maps the human/nature divide onto the male/female divide. Because of the capacities and roles of their bodies in the process of reproduction, women are associated with the natural world—identified as that which, without conscious or rational human intervention, simply happens in the same way over and over again. The impulse or desire to have sex and thus create new human life is also naturalized, something that simply happens because nature made it so. Thus, reproductive events (menstruation, sex, conception, gestation, birth, and caregiving) are natural; the historical and cultural meanings they accumulate in different times and spaces are trivial and "personal." They do not make changes in history; they are that upon which history, defined as male activity, acts. Modernity, with its scientific values and capitalist economies, requires and even celebrates the dominance of man over nature. Since "woman" is categorized as/with nature, the dominance of woman and nature is necessary for human progress.

As will be seen below, most feminist policy approaches attempt to detach "woman" from her ideological and socialized identification with nature and caregiving, challenging this as a rationale for male dominance. These frameworks for policy seek to overturn or eliminate the association of women and reproduction with nature, minimizing the impact of this association on women's capacities to participate in the formal economy, or to eliminate altogether the dualisms of public/private space, the formal/informal economies, and the individual/nuclear family.

In contrast, ecofeminists engaged with environmental politics and policy have embraced woman's association with nature. To challenge masculinist principles of competition over and with nature and rejections of association with the natural, "feminine" principles are elevated. Whether because of religious belief or historical socialization, women of all ages and in all places care for others in pursuing the necessities of reproduction, which require guaranteed sources of water, food, and shelter, not contingent, state-offered, or market-driven access. Ecofeminists argue principles identified with the femininized body, character, and history elevate care over competition and sustainability (re-producibility) over profit-driven growth. Mobilizing women who identify as women is critical to all feminist policy frameworks, but ecofeminists argue these principles are essentially feminine in nature. Ecofeminist mobilization is akin to a spiritual and organic quest more so than a political and historical one.

Ecofeminists have influenced policy, engaging with macro political dynamics through the United Nations, the World Bank, and other global institutions in addition to working on the state and local levels. They developed global environmental actions opposing World Bank development campaigns in the 1980s and advocating for pro-subsistence farming campaigns that would radically mitigate climate change. Vandana Shiva, a leading voice identified with the transnational ecofeminist movement, has focused attention on the production of food. She leads movements against genetically modified organisms (GMO) and the private patenting of seeds. She argues for devaluing industry and biotechnology and for (re)valuing what ecofeminism identifies as traditional, natural, organic processes. Women suffer rather than benefit from extractive and high-tech forms of industrial farming. Scientific and industrial/capitalist strategies for managing and controlling the food supply interfere with what ecofeminists identify as indigenous, organic knowledge of how to grow food by tending to the soil in a sustainable fashion. Ecofeminists want to put food production in the hands of those who have a closer connection to the natural world and thus know how to grow food in ways that counter destructive modernization strategies.

This kind of argument is criticized on the grounds of whether what Shiva calls "subsistence agriculture" can feed the millions upon millions of people now inhabiting the Earth, and whether the dangers claimed about GMO food and the harmful outcomes of privatized seed production are verifiable. Debates more specific to feminist policy frameworks center on whether ecofeminist arguments simply reproduce dualisms of man/woman as mapped here onto science/nature. Ecofeminism argues biotechnologies and any version of industrialized farming, whether for profit or not-for-profit, are inherently damaging because they assume man must master the Earth and do not respect the feminine principles of closeness to and care for the Earth and its bounty. As Shiva has said, "GMO" stands for "God Move Over."[5] This communicates the spiritual and anti-science grounds on which the ecofeminist movement, as synthesized in her analyses and work, stands.

Feminists critical of ecofeminism argue that the masculine/feminine dualism is itself a product of patriarchal power and, as Audre Lorde famously said, that we cannot use the master's tools to take apart the master's house. Deploying it in reverse credits what is a first principle of patriarchy: that gender is a binary in which one side relies on its superiority to the other for its integrity and legitimacy. Further, it is fair to ask whether the "natural" can ever again be known or experienced in what is now commonly agreed is the epoch of the Anthropocene—a historical moment in which the human impact on the planet is irrevocably changing the planet.[6]

However, in part because they have generated such fierce debate, the theory and kinds of activism in which ecofeminists have engaged have contributed to scaling attention to gender to a global level with respect to studies of and policies about farming and food production. Feminist researchers not allied with ecofeminism have done empirical studies since the 1980s showing that women have fewer options when climate crises hit communities and, being the primary caregivers, are deeply burdened as they take responsibility for the wellbeing of children and elderly people. Linkages have been made to educational opportunities for women and their capacities to make autonomous choices about childbearing and raising, which in turn are related to environmental issues of the Earth's capacities. And, with reference to the earlier discussion of farming, studies focused on the agricultural gender gap indicate that if women had equal access to productive resources to men, they could increase their production by 20%–30%, feeding an additional 150 million people.[7]

There are hundreds of intersectional transnational feminist environmental projects seeking to research and model different ways of living with and in the environment and practice healthy, ecologically sustainable relationships. Ecofeminism—a term describing a more complex set of framings than I can do justice to in this brief introduction—has been influential in encouraging feminists and others concerned with the environment and climate change to think about actual human beings in relationship to nature, and the differences among us as to how we relate to and engage with the natural world, no matter how it is constructed in different times and places. While we should avoid romanticizing any particular groups or historical moment in the context of relating to nature, we can develop and act on principles that respect what has been associated with the feminine and femininity. Reclaiming some of the meanings attached to and the practices of those who identify or are identified as women in the world and extending them into the public space may help us live differently without reproducing patriarchal dualisms of man-public/woman-private or male-culture/female-nature and the injustices inherent in the attendant valuations of each side.

ANTI-DISCRIMINATION POLICIES IN THE WORK-FORCE AND EDUCATIONAL INSTITUTIONS

This section discusses equality and equity and how feminists have thought about and acted against discrimination on the basis of sex. I focus on feminist politics and policymaking in the US, where liberalism remains the dominant frame. Equality is a concept central to discussions of Western liberal political theory. In the 17th and 18th centuries, social contract theorists argued, in response to monarchic systems of rule, that in a state of nature, each individual human being is endowed by God or by nature with an innate right to self-preservation and the capacity for reason. Political organization must acknowledge this by refusing monarchic values that distribute power and resources by birthright and tradition rather than by individual right and merit. Equity is a contemporary concept invoked as an alternative to equality as the aspiration of feminist movements. As explained below, use of this term signals an activist and redistributive approach to confronting discrimination. Individual rights and merit are too detached from material and historical reality to effectively counter the ways unjust structures and systems have positioned us in radically different places when it comes to achieving socioeconomic parity and social recognition for our accomplishments and talents.

Thinking back to discussions in Chapter 2 about feminisms that engage with liberalism, remember how tightly bound liberal arguments about equality are to abstract individualism, but also to property defined as "private." Individuals are endowed (alternatively by God or by nature) with reason; they do not require one another to cultivate that capacity. This inherent reasonableness leads them to pre-determined conclusions about why they may lay claim to themselves, their labor, and the stuff they produce and/or transform in nature. The self becomes a property not to be interfered with by systems of governance, and the property that self acquires (e.g., land, wealth) also lies in the "private" space, outside of government interference.

These entrenched values render the unequal distribution of and access to resources as "normal" because every person is expected to be responsible for their own accumulation (if not preservation, in the sense of protection from others—liberalism does rely on the state for that) of property. We are not all the same in our capacity or desire to accumulate stuff, so the results will necessarily be different for each. Feminists have fought hard over the last century to have people identified as women recognized as invested with the most basic rights to the autonomy and opportunity to accumulate and be protected from harm that liberalism sets out.

Title VII of the Civil Rights Act of 1964, in the iteration that first came to the floor of Congress, forbade discrimination against individuals on the basis of race, color, religion, or national origin. "Sex" was added to the list as a "poison pill," meaning legislators opposed to the Civil Rights Act put it in the bill in hopes it would therefore not pass. It nonetheless passed by a wide majority and Lyndon Johnson signed it into law.

The Equal Employment Opportunity Commission (EEOC) is the agency created by Congress and directed by the President to enforce the Civil Rights Act. It was the utter lack of attention to sex discrimination by the executive branch that inspired feminist women, many of whom were attorneys, to create the National Organization for Women (NOW). NOW initially organized to pressure President Lyndon Johnson to include "sex" in the language of policies shaping enforcement of the Civil Rights Act. While sex was finally written into a new executive order in 1967, the EEOC continued to ignore sex discrimination in its enforcement efforts. Ultimately, policies governed by the Civil Rights Act had to work in conjunction with legal challenges brought on the grounds that discrimination on the basis of sex violated the equal protection clause of the 14th Amendment to the US Constitution.

Feminist attorneys worked diligently to make the system recognize "discrimination on the basis of sex" as an actionable claim (meaning courts would accept women's complaints rather than dismissing them out of hand). It was not an easy or a straightforward path. As Ruth Bader Ginsberg was establishing the Women's Rights Project of the American Civil Liberties Union, she shaped anti-discrimination law in the US by strategically bringing a case about discrimination against a male. In *Morris v Commissioners of the IRS*,[8] the Court ruled, for the first time, that discrimination on the basis of sex was a violation of the 14th Amendment.

Feminist policy reformers worked to pass the Civil Rights Act of 1991 allowing for jury trials and compensatory damages in cases about harassment and discrimination. The Lily Ledbetter Act of 2009 allows plaintiffs to sue on the basis of each incident of discrimination—in this case, each paycheck given to a woman that was significantly less than those given to the men in similar sites of employment. These advances in anti-discrimination law vastly expanded the potential for anti-discrimination lawsuits, opening doors for women to the workplace and educational institutions.

Policies that use state power to force institutions and employers not to discriminate are enforcing basic tenets of the Western liberal tradition. Yet the word "sex" as included in Title VII has led to complicated debates about the meaning of "sex." For example, the response to sex discrimination claims was applied to the question of whether height and weight restrictions constitute a legitimate Bonafide Occupational Qualification (BFOQ). This was challenged in 1977 in a case known as *Dothard v. Rawlinson*[9] by a woman denied a position as a prison guard as she did not meet the height requirement. The Supreme Court ruled that the weight and height requirements, which would apply to 41% of women, were not proper BFOQs, but that it was appropriate for the state to deny women positions in maximum-security male prisons because of security and safety concerns. Here, sex discrimination is prohibited if size and weight are used as measures (not the anatomy of a person). Yet it perpetuates assumptions about essential differences between men and women, the latter of whom are not safe around males convicted of criminal acts (because of anatomy).

A civil harm now identified around the globe as sexual harassment took over 20 years to be accepted by courts as actionable under Title VII. Sexualized behavior and commentary in workplaces were historically (and too often still are) understood to be about sex as desire; understood as flirting and perhaps immoral, they did not constitute illegal behavior. Instead, this was personal (see Chapter 4). Feminist attorneys took on the project of showing that sexualized behavior in the public space is not about "sex" in the sense of desire or potentially consensual activity. Rather, they argued, it has always been about the abuse of power by some over others. Sex harassment became part of the legal lexicon as arguments that if "sex" was used as a *quid pro quo* scheme (e.g., sexual favors in exchange for a pay raise) or was shown to create a hostile working environment (preventing some from flourishing equally in the workplace due to their membership of a particular group), victims could sue under Title VII and the equal protection clause of the 14th Amendment (*Meritor Savings Bank v. Vinson*).[10] In *Harris v. Forklift Systems* (1993),[11] the Supreme Court built on *Meritor*, ruling that a plaintiff need not provide evidence of physical or psychological harm to claim sex harassment.

In *Oncale v. Sundowner Services* (1995),[12] same-sex harassment was identified by the court as actionable under Title VII and the 14th Amendment. The Court held that "sex" in this case did not have to mean harassment of a differently sexed person. It could mean any sexualized behavior that places an employee in a disadvantageous position. "Sex" here is any sexualized behavior targeting another person and creating a condition of disadvantage (inequality). It need not be enacted because of a difference between men and women.

Thus, "sex"—an apparently simple reference—is jurisprudentially parsed; its complicated and multiple meanings, long understood and articulated by feminists concerned with male dominance, were embedded in liberal legal culture. Generally, to call what had been associated with merely personal interactions an abuse of power and control was a tectonic shift in expectations of how "sex" was enacted in the workplace. "Sex" as spoken or physical behavior, and linked to expectations of gendered identities, became a site of legal contestation.

These ongoing developments in what "sex" means in Title VII indicates the malleability of this category more generally. Race, religion, ethnicity and other ascriptive identities are not so ambiguous. These differences do not make it any easier or more difficult to win discrimination cases. The Supreme Court, having become more conservative since the 1990s, has narrowed the field by focusing on intent rather than outcome in looking at discrimination cases. In other words, there must be intent on the part of an employee to discriminate. Cases focusing on patterns and practices or outcome are no longer as successful.

Following in the classical liberal tradition, Title VII and 14th Amendment jurisprudence makes clear that equality of opportunity must be available to all. Federal and state anti-discrimination laws require that there be no barriers to every individual competing based on their skills and capacities as an individual. Ascriptive categories of race or sex or ethnicity should not be barriers to opportunity to participate in educational institutions, workplaces, or other non-private spaces. The basic limitations to this approach to achieving equality, however, is that it is not about the systems that create the discrimination in the first place: white supremacy and patriarchal dominance in the public space. It is about individuals being willing to put their jobs and life purpose on the line to go to court. The efforts to change legal doctrine have been long and hard; and while the feminist legal movement has traveled that bumpy road for years, different strategies to reach the ends of equality in the way liberals think about it have also emerged.

THE CONTEMPORARY SHIFT TO "EQUITY"

With studies showing only very incremental improvement in outcomes for groups historically discriminated against, there has been a shift in the discursive framing of anti-discrimination policies. The term "equity" is now so common as to be a kind of mantra among those attempting to make opportunities not only available but accessible to all kinds of people. Part of this shift can be interpreted as being driven by an increasingly conservative response to legal challenges to discrimination. While individuals can still challenge discrimination, increasingly conservative courts in the US since the 1980s have made even these modest initiatives more difficult—for example, demanding plaintiffs (those alleging discrimination) prove intent on the part of the company or institution rather than using patterns of practice and outcomes as evidence. Feminist legal reform advocates struggle to give evidence when discrimination is not overt. We know that the civil rights and women's movements changed how race and sex are spoken about. Discriminatory sentiments and practices are less overt, but still present. They can be seen in demographic analyses of the workforce and practices carried on in the workplace or educational institution that preclude or inhibit in subtle ways full participation by all. This has been identified as "implicit bias." While implicit bias is the subject of workplace and educational workshops, it is not yet commonly recognized by courts as evidence of discrimination.

Rather than relying on the courts to adjudicate discrimination after the fact, feminists use the language of equity to refer to the conditions *from which and into which* individuals are entering the workplace or educational opportunities. The reference to "equity" argues that each person must be given what they require to approach the doors cracked opened by anti-discrimination laws and then be fully capacitated while there.

A popular way to explain the difference between "equality" and "equity" used by those advocating equity-driven redistributive policies shows three persons of different heights trying to look over a fence at a baseball game. "Equality" means they will all be given the same-sized box to stand on to look over the fence. "Equity" means they will each be given a box that, according to their height, will allow them to look over the fence. Some feminists will take this story at face value and argue that differences among us make different resources necessary if those who are, in this case, of smaller stature are to have a chance at an opportunity in the first place. Equity then means ensuring an individual who is of the first generation of their family to attend college has support filling out federal financial aid forms or, when they arrive at campus, has specialized orientation sessions. In general, equity—differently from equality—facilitates entry once a person is on the road toward an opportunity and facilitates fair treatment once they have walked (or fought their way) through the door into the institution.

Feminists who are critical of the equality and equity policy approaches argue they limit our vision of justice because they focus on individuals surviving/living in the social order racialized, patriarchal capitalism requires. Neither the equality nor the equity framework for policymaking requires changes in the conditions from which a person or group comes—conditions that may or may not make it possible for them to get on the road to the opportunity in the first place. They may ask why the person in fact requires a taller box, but their solutions are about getting them the box and on the box, not changing the conditions that require a box in the first place. They do not examine whether access to jobs or the additional resources will simply give groups and individuals opportunities to participate in an unjust set of practices or system. They do not ask who built the fence or why. Is the fence a signifier of private property and exclusion or a signifier of protection? Protection from what/whom? Some might say, "Let's abolish the fence," but still not ask whether/why the figures want or should want whatever it is behind the fence in the first place. Equality and equity policies are argued to be ameliorative, not transformative. These critical responses indicate that feminisms should challenge not only "inequality" or "inequity" but the context in which the institutions in which we seek equity thrive. Institutions themselves are not neutral spaces being filled up by different kinds of people. Like in the example of the fence and the baseball game, the gendered/raced/classed/ableist qualities of the institutions we aspire to join, the spectacle we want to look at, must also be called into question.

Further, feminists critical of liberalism show equality or equity in this view means becoming "like" those who are successful in a competitive capitalist environment sustained by what critics show to be disembodied (dismissive of material or embodied conditions) reason and the punitive capacities (not the reasonable persuasive-ness) of law. Equality in this view implies individuals achieve their own success and status as privatized selves, not selves deeply embedded in enabling or disenabling structures; not selves who are essentially interdependent upon others. Liberalism of this ilk does not allow discrimination on the basis of attributes or identities or beliefs that have no relevance to the opportunity on offer. In the US, an example of a law that reflects this version of liberalism, and which feminist-identified women worked to pass and still work to enforce, is Title VII of the Civil Rights Act of 1964. I use this as the primary example in this section as it has been central to rights orga-nizations' efforts to establish women's equality under law. While minimal in terms of eliminating basic barriers to equal representa-tion in public institutions and the workplace, it continues to be a struggle to make even this ameliorative policy work for women.

GENDERED QUOTAS IN POLITICAL REPRESENTATION

The equality/equity discussion is related to debates about getting more women into positions of power and influence within govern-ment institutions. When we think about equality/equity, we might refer to how many women are elected to, are appointed to, or work in government institutions in various positions and at different levels. In the US, this is discussed in terms of whether women should empha-size their gender, racial, and/or ethnic identity as they campaign; this debate focuses our attention on demographics, or what kinds of peo-ple are in what kinds of positions of power and influence. However, "quotas" generally—in hiring, in educational institutions, and in government—are deeply unpopular in the US. The US is more indi-vidualist in its political culture than other countries. Internationally, over 130 countries have implemented quota systems, voluntary and involuntary, for recruiting and supporting women to campaign for and/or be appointed to political and executive offices in government. Feminists generally support this strategy, but that support translates into many different ideas about why and how to argue for quotas. Quota systems have also come and gone from many electoral sys-tems, allowing for studies to be carried out about the impact of differ-ent kinds of quota systems on gender and politics.

WHY QUOTAS?

If we rely on the binary woman/man to count heads, women constitute over half the adult population worldwide. Yet in 2021, women held only 17 out of 151 positions as heads of state (presidents), 19 out of 193 positions as heads of governments (parliaments), and 22.8% of all ministerial positions (close advisers and top executive administrators). Drilling down, we see that when it comes to appointments to executive positions in government (cabinet ministries and the like), women are more likely to be appointed to environmental, educational, or human and social rights positions, while men continue to be appointed to positions related to finance, war, justice, and diplomacy. These latter positions determine outcomes with respect to flows of money and the means of violence, internationally and domestically. They tend to have more power and influence than the "domestic" ministries. In legislative branches, women hold 26.5% of all seats. If we again drill down to local institutions of governance, we find women in about 35% of elected positions.

Thus, feminists who advocate for quotas argue that we need to attend to basic fairness in the general numbers of women and men in positions of power from top to bottom in government institutions (elective and administrative), workforces, and educational institutions. For some, it is about the basic principle that governing bodies should look like the population they serve. Going a bit deeper, arguments for quotas are about getting to a "critical mass" whereby women who are elected or appointed are no longer "tokens" and are no longer required to engage with masculinist environments as heroic individuals. On the one hand, we wish to normalize the presence of women in positions of influence and power; on the other hand, we must continue to think critically about the positions and institutions themselves and whether the mere presence of female bodies makes a difference in all women's lives.

HOW ARE QUOTAS IMPLEMENTED?

Quota policies do not pay attention to the policy preferences or ideology of the candidates; nor do they pay attention to candidates' backgrounds. They simply set aside seats for people who identify as women in spaces where positions of influence and power are held by, if not formally reserved for, men. Quotas can be voluntary, like in Sweden, meaning there are terms set out in law allowing but not requiring quotas to be met in the holding of seats in parliament. Or they may be mandatory, as in India, where women must sit in a certain number of elected seats. Quotas can be instituted by political parties as they recruit candidates or by governments as they set aside seats in parliament for women, thus requiring parties to recruit and support those women.

There is an important difference between "winner-take-all" electoral systems, like that which exists in the United States, and proportional systems, like those which exist in parliamentary democracies such as Sweden and Germany. Quotas are generally more effective in democracies governed by proportional representation. In parliamentary systems, the *party* wins elections and then appoints the number of candidates to seats according to the percentage of the vote received generally. In this kind of system, it is a little easier to replace men with women as candidates because voters are electing a governing party, not the individuals running for office. US elections focus less on party affiliation and more on the individual characteristics of the candidates. Quota systems work better in parliamentary systems in which parties have more control than individual candidates. Sexism and misogyny against candidates who are women have less impact in defining the terms on which electoral contests are won or lost.

Studies on quotas indicate that establishing quota systems should not simply be regarded as "common sense" to feminists. We should look carefully at what is accomplished and what women continue to face as gendered subjects. Studies on Swedish parliamentarians show that women in those seats are generally more educated and more qualified in terms of work experience than the men. They also reveal that when higher numbers of women hold positions of power, no matter their ideological preferences, "women's issues" receive more attention. Yet research on the Swedish experience further shows that women in Swedish governance continue to report high levels of sexual harassment and abuse as they do their work as parliamentarians.[13] In other words, even a significant percentage of women coming into the room—what I called a "critical mass"—may not be enough to shift the deeply entrenched misogyny informing the sense of masculinist prerogative among male colleagues. Again, context matters. The systems into which women enter require transformation even as quotas make it possible for previously excluded groups to enter.

Another example comes from India, where quotas are mandatory on a rotating basis across regional governments. Studies show that reporting of sexualized acts of violence increase when women hold more seats. However, and offering more evidence that intersectionality is essential to all feminist thinking about all issues, it is also clear from the research that the reporting of sexual harms did not reach across caste assignment.[14] Women who were already among the privileged in non-gendered ways in their communities were elected, and women who were already among the privileged in non-gendered ways showed an increased willingness to report sexualized harms committed against them.

Quota systems are a blunt instrument when it comes to struggling for gender justice; some feminists refer to them as "efficient" ways of getting more women into political office. It may be that the more women, the less masculinity can hover over, dominate, hegemonize, and rule in the public space. However, feminist critics of quotas argue that we should assess candidates for positions of power and influence by how they enact their gender in relationship to others and how they think about gendered issues, rather than whether they identify with one gender or the other (this latter discussion assumes a binary definition of "gender" as man/woman). For example, Margaret Thatcher, the long-serving Prime Minister of Britain (1979–1990), was consistently covered by the media as a woman. Her comportment and status as a woman were paid constant attention. While her presence and behavior as a woman were examined, often in sexist and demeaning ways, she nonetheless worked against the interests of women across the board, with the hardest hit being women in immigrant communities and working-class women. In general, Thatcher was deeply influential in initiating the swing to conservatism and anti-feminist agitation and policies in Western politics that began in the 1980s.

Framing debate around quota systems often means we dither over whether we should support a person because she is identified as or identifies herself as a woman. Candidates are consistently faced with strategic decisions and often caught in a bind about whether or how to discuss, proclaim, or enact their identity as a woman on the campaign trail or in office. The enactment or imitation of masculinist comportment and habits is entrenched as a qualification for public service, in the economy, government, and education. Given the deep association of masculinity with what is valued in the public space, such as competition, individualism, and abstract reasoning, feminists critical of prioritizing quotas want to go deeper than electing more women to positions of power and influence. They suggest that feminist argument, discourse, claims-making, and activism—no matter the gender identity of the speaker/activist—will ultimately change the masculinist character of the public space.

Critics claim quotas may be a distraction since gender identity is no guarantee of belief or action. Further, once more people identified as women are in positions of power, sexism and gender dominance may appear to be less of an issue even while the majority of women's experiences are shaped by them. It may be surprising that quota systems are controversial among feminists. However, remember that feminism does not take the category of "woman" for granted in thinking about how to make progress toward gender justice. No one who argues for quotas says they are a panacea, but whether they get us closer to gender justice must be carefully considered.

REPRODUCTIVE JUSTICE

> One of the singular features of our movement is that we are weaving abortion into a web of other political issues.
>
> Verónica Gago[15]

Feminists have fought for autonomy in the context of the reproductive lives of all persons with the capacity to be pregnant. This includes demands that governments make access to whatever is necessary for reproductive autonomy before, during, and after pregnancy to be a reality, not merely an abstract right.[16] In struggles about birth control, abortion, unequal access to healthcare, discriminatory habits in research agendas across the spectrum of gendered identifications, the medicalization and surveillance of pregnancy, and childcare, feminists have worked to articulate and argued among themselves about strategies and what reproductive justice looks like in terms of policy. There is no disagreement among feminists that the capacity of those who identify as women, transgender, or non-binary individuals to gestate fetuses and give birth has made their bodies battlegrounds for control by patriarchal systems. When reproductive autonomy is denied, bodies and lives are being put to theological, cultural, social or political ends. There is also a hard-fought consensus among contemporary feminists that the liberal understanding of abortion as an isolated "choice" is too limited. The "rights" and "privacy" framework set out by the landmark Supreme Court decision in *Roe v. Wade* of 1973 establishing abortion as a constitutional right was ultimately overruled in 2022. While it defined the movement in the US, it was clear well before the ruling in *Dobbs v. Jackson Women's Health* overturned the 1973 decision that *Roe* was an inadequate protection for women, girls, and trans-gendered and non-binary people who wanted accessible care to end their pregnancies. The liberal rights framework of privacy is subject to override by patriarchal powers as "fetal rights" or the "rights of the unborn" are set against rights to autonomy and the medical care anyone who is pregnant requires in order to continue or to end a pregnancy.[17]

The feminist framework of reproductive justice is about more than individual rights; it speaks to the material conditions that shape our reproductive lives and may lead to the need for and access to abortion. Importantly, however, it extends feminists' concerns to the conditions in which families, no matter who claims to be a family or kin, can thrive. Abortion is integrated into the "web of other political issues," including historical oppressions that impact different groups of those who can get pregnant in very different ways.

The right to and access to abortions at various stages of pregnancy under various conditions do not exhaust the category of reproductive autonomy, though the basic injustice of and catastrophic effects of denying abortion rights have focused attention on abortion itself in places with conservative laws. The theory and action of the reproductive justice movement have expanded what has been traditionally known among feminists as the "right to abortion" into a movement in which women's reproductive health is considered holistically and understood in all of the complex political/cultural contexts in which people who give birth and care for others exist.

Feminists with an intersectional and transnationalist focus show that the right to abortion must be understood as one demand among others that together will realize reproductive justice for all women in all contexts. Women of color and from the Global South have criticized the mostly white-led abortion rights movement in Western countries for being too focused on protecting the right to abortion, which does not guarantee or protect actual access to abortion care and, more importantly, fails to recognize how abortion is only one possibility in our reproductive lives. As did white suffragists with respect to voting and middle-class white feminists with respect to anti-discrimination policy, the mainstream abortion rights movement fails to see how women of color fall through the cracks of race, ethnicity, and socioeconomic status when it comes to their reproductive lives. Dorothy Roberts[18] shows this when she discusses civil rights leaders who argued birth control and abortion are akin to genocide against Black people in the US. Black male leaders commonly argued that Black women should become pregnant and give birth to lift up the Black race. She also argues that abortion is only one aspect of the deprivations of bodily and reproductive autonomy inflicted on Black women. Abortion rights cannot be separated from forced sterilization, compelled contraception, or the hyper-enforcement of child welfare laws against Black families.

With respect to abortion itself, feminists emphasize a startling fact: on average, fewer abortions are performed per pregnancy (34/1000) in countries that permit abortion than in those that prohibit abortion (37/1000).[19] This indicates that criminalizing abortion does not reduce the number of abortions; it only harms those who seek them because the medical care is not legal, accessible, or safe. Furthermore, countries with strict restrictions on abortion will also have strict restrictions on birth control and conservative policies about sex education, so more unplanned pregnancies will result. For feminists, this is evidence that criminalizing abortion is not about "helping women" (anti-abortion movements do not recognize trans or non-binary people) or "saving both lives," as the anti-abortion movement in Argentina, among others, insists. It is about controlling those identified as or who identify as women and girls' sexuality and denying them reproductive autonomy no matter the outcomes.

The abortion rights movement emerged in the US as radical and left-wing women detached from the male-dominated social movements of the 1960s that persistently marginalized and trivialized women's voices and concerns particular to gender dynamics. The first formal speak-out (a means by which to make otherwise "private" or personal experiences a matter for public concern) of the feminist movement of the latter half of the 20th century was about abortion. In 1969, a feminist organization called Redstockings organized a protest during a New York Assembly committee hearing about liberalizing abortion laws. The only woman scheduled to formally testify at the hearing was a nun deeply opposed to abortion. Members of Redstockings refused to leave the building until they were heard and, when accused of personal pique against men (because they were asking to speak as women), stated clearly that it was not personal pique but political grievance that inspired them. Since that time, feminists globally have used speak-outs to make stories of the personal pain and suffering of unwanted or dangerous pregnancies part of the public debate about whether abortion should be legal. Feminists have also focused on showing that people who are pregnant seek to end their pregnancies no matter the law, and that access to medically safe abortions is a matter not only of life and death but of autonomy or servitude.

While the movement for abortion rights emerged in the late 1960s in the US, feminist histories of abortion show that it has always been a part of reproductive life in every kind of community. Abortion was formally criminalized across the globe in the late 19th and early 20th century. Despite the criminal status of abortion, the early women's health and women's rights movements worked to help women to find trustworthy doctors for the procedure and to teach women to administer abortions themselves. The most famous network of this kind in the US was known as the Jane Collective in Chicago, Illinois, which focused on helping poor women find and pay for abortion care. Rickie Solinger, among other historians of abortion, also show that for women who could afford to travel or pay doctors, abortion was easily accessible. In Argentina, for example, the state turned a blind eye if it was a privileged women requiring the medical service. Argentine feminists identify this as the privileged males protecting "their" women while feeling free to judge and control the actions of the vulnerable classes.

In the US, in 1973, the Supreme Court issued its landmark *Roe v. Wade* ruling, identifying abortion as a privacy right but simultaneously saying that states have an increasing interest in the "life of the fetus" with each passing trimester of a pregnancy. This allowed states to constrain and even ban access to abortion, often with little concern for the health or life of the mother, later in the pregnancy. The right to and access to abortion have been systematically weakened ever since *Roe v. Wade* was handed down. For example, in 1992, the line determining the state's interest in limiting women's right to abortion became "viability" (set at 24 weeks) and strict limitations on access such as requiring parental consent or a judicial waiver, requiring clinics to have association with hospitals or requiring the clinics themselves to mimic hospital conditions, flourished across the states. The history of regulation and policing of abortion since *Roe v. Wade* makes clear that abortion conceived as an individual right under a privacy framework is not an adequate framing. It is, in fact, exclusionary as it fails to establish abortion as an essential aspect of reproductive healthcare and, importantly, essential for establishing the *equal citizenship* of women.

While among the first to liberalize, the US has radically backtracked even from the very limited promise of reproductive rights. In June 2022, the US Supreme Court overturned *Roe v. Wade*, reversing earlier law that said abortion was a right under the privacy doctrine. The need for feminists to move beyond the individual rights and privacy framework could not be clearer. Examples from Argentina and Ireland offer further evidence. In Argentina, class politics and the hypocrisy of the Catholic Church in ignoring its own support for a militarist dictatorship and abusive priests while claiming it advocated for the "life of both" the woman and the unborn child dominated the discourse leading up to the momentous liberalization of abortion laws in 2020. Feminist analyses of the Argentine movement embed the moment of 2020 in the deep context of feminist movements since the 1970s, thus showing how reproductive justice movements—even beyond the success of legalization—must engage in the "web of other political issues." Also in 2020, the Irish legislature passed legislation activating the repeal of the 8th Amendment to the Irish Constitution, which supported the rights of the fetus, prohibiting abortion except when the life of the woman or girl was at stake.

The extreme dangers and burdens of unwanted pregnancies or those that threaten the health of the individual who is pregnant tend to focus attention on the urgent right of access to abortion care. However, feminist reproductive justice activists argue for an expanded vision; the movement for reproductive justice attends to the panoply of issues related to women's reproductive lives. Who is seeking abortions and why? Is it that they do not have access to birth control? Are they victims of sexual violence? Are they socio-economically stressed? Do they want to be mothers and what is their sense of that identity? SisterSong,[20] as a leading organization in the reproductive justice movement, identifies women's autonomy as embodied subjects, the right of people to have or not have children, and the basic conditions necessary to raise children in safe and sustainable communities as human rights. Identifying these as human rights internationalizes the discourse and demands global scrutiny of policies implemented by any particular nation-state. More pragmatically, it focuses attention on what it takes to sustain reproductive autonomy, which includes not only abortion, but conditions that enable healthy gestation, birth, and the raising of children. While the basic right to abortion is critical to this, it does not exhaust the complexity of reproductive life. As I said in introducing this section, feminists agree about the need to support reproductive autonomy; discussions and debates among feminists are about strategy, what to pay attention to and how to articulate the complexity of policy analyses and prescriptions, drawing out connections between abortion rights and the other needs and rights of those who become pregnant, who give birth, and who are primary caregivers at so many levels in most places. Some feminists add to that list a demand that caregiving labor be intentionally redistributed across genders. Others argue that if resources demanded by reproductive justice movements are made available, equitable caregiving practices will occur. They argue that reproductive justice will lessen the burden and increase understanding that caregiving is a public good, not only a private obligation. In working toward reproductive justice, feminists focus simultaneously on caregiving as a public good and the normalization of abortion as healthcare.

SEXUALIZED VIOLENCE

Feminists have politicized sexual violence—a kind of violence that is very personal in its impact and deeply stigmatized culturally— through activism and theorizing. We should note that rape and other forms of physical sexualized abuse have generally been identified by mainstream culture as unacceptable. However, the grounds on which sexual violence is unacceptable in any particular time or place have been typically defined by the patriarchal moral values dominant in any given community, not by generalized principles of respect for the bodily integrity, wellbeing, and autonomy of each person. For example, as early as 1641, in the Puritan colony of Massachusetts, what we now call "domestic violence" was punished at the whipping post and rape was sometimes punished by banishment or death. However, it was punished only when sexualized violence or wife and child abuse was identified as an insult or dishonor against the man to whom the women and children "belonged" (in the pre-revolutionary colonies, following in the common law tradition of couverture defined in Chapter 1, family members identified as female were the property of the male in the household) or the community within which the victim was embedded. Only some women were subject to these protections. Wives and women who were enslaved were not considered raped if the perpetrator was the husband/master. Sex workers were identified as unrapable because they sold sex and thus consented to making their bodies available. Single women were considered available for sex. Further, thinking about sexual violence in moral terms constructs it as an individual failing on the part of the perpetrator or, as is more common, on the part of the victim, rather than a systematically normalized threat under patriarchal conditions.

Feminists argue that sexual violence must register publicly as a political, not a moral issue. Sexual violence is the imposition and perpetuation of dominance and control over feminized bodies. Catharine MacKinnon takes this analysis further in arguing that perpetrators of sexual violence are having what they experience as sex; they "get sex" by means of coercion if the person they want to have sex with says no at any given point of the encounter.[21] Perpetrators learn from what feminists have called "rape culture" that in sex, "no" is not real or can/should change during an encounter to a "maybe" or a "yes." In some contexts, the response of the other person is not accounted for at all. They are there for purposes of sex, so sex is "had" with them. And, of course, some perpetrators are enacting what they know to be violence. In these cases, it is sheer sexual dominance over a sexualized other that drives the rape or abuse. Feminists argue there is no moral failing here in the sense that the aggressor's violence and coercion register within the readings of the moral compass offered them by the gendered order of things. Patriarchal moralizing about rape only references certain women who "belong" to certain men or communities.

Much feminist work on law and policy has been done through the criminal courts. When sexual violence has been reported and reaches the system currently in place to adjudicate harms—the criminal legal system—the moral failing narrative attached to victims comes into sharp relief. Here the issue is not what the perpetrator thought or did, but that the law and communities focus on where the victim was, how they were dressed, what messages they communicated, and whether they resisted in a way that would prove they did not want to have sex. Children who are abused are made to think it is their attractiveness, behavior, or failure to resist that is to blame for the violence. Women and girls are asked how much sex they have had and with whom, why they were in that place at that time, and whether/how they resisted, physically or with words. Women, girls, and feminized others are told it is their responsibility to avoid or stop the violence. Their moral character as a gendered subject becomes the issue, as they are typically required to show that they do not want to have sex generally, not just with that person at that time.

Other ways sexualized violence becomes the victim's responsibility in mainstream legal and cultural narratives reference the dynamics of desire and the inherent vulnerability and thus availability of the femininized figure. It is due to a woman's frigidity or confusion if she does not want to have sex with a person she is married to or if she wants to stop sex after indicating desire at some moment in an encounter. When men and boys are abused, they are identified as weak, which is equated with being effeminate or feminine. No matter the gender/sex of the victim, they are feminized and face moral interrogation and cultural norms that work against recognition of a serious harm or accountability for the perpetrator. Feminist legal reformers have fought for rape shield laws, the repeal of marital exemption statutes (including those that say spouses may not testify against one another), and more education and training for police and prosecutors about the dynamics of sexual violence and abuse.

Identifying sexual violence as a moral failing on the part of the perpetrator or the victim makes the violence a community issue that might be addressed by introducing a law or a policy. But whether the moralizing gaze is on the accused or one the victim, this lens obscures the dynamics of power and dominance that make sexual violence so common. Feminists have rendered sexual violence a political issue precisely by speaking out about the harms done to women and children as individuals in terms of their individual lives and wellbeing, but also by way of claims about structural dominance, masculinist privilege, and heterosexism—all of which are implicated in perpetuating sexual violence in most times and places.

Sexualized violence takes many forms. Sexual harassment, rape, and domestic abuse are the three contemporary categories constructed and worked on by policymakers over the last 60 years. We mentioned earlier that Swedish women who hold office in parliament, while making up a majority, still experience sexual harassment and abuse.[22] This tells us that men assume their prerogative in the public space. Because the vast majority of perpetrators identify as male, all cases of sexual harassment and abuse—whether against male or female or non-binary bodies—show how this is the case. Men have been dominant in what most social orders call the public space of decision-making, not universally, but for the most part, across time and space. Sometimes discourse will reflect the assumptions that governed gender roles explicitly through the 19th century: that women have "power" in the private space ("She rules the household; I do what she tells me") while failing to see that male access to power in the public space ultimately defines that private space (sets the contractual terms of marriage, rules on custody of children, control of the money, and distribution of resources). This sense among men that women exist in a parallel universe to the spaces in which men hold institutionalized power impacts how they think about women who enter "their" space. If women enter the public space—whether that be the street, the workplace, or institutions of government—they do so as figures with whom "private" interactions remain appropriate. The figure of the woman is an intrusion into the public space; sexual harassment confirms men's dominance of the public space when females or femininized figures happen into it. As mentioned above, as part of the fight for equality, sexual harassment has been redefined by feminists as discriminatory—as a means by which women and feminized figures are prevented from becoming colleagues or workers because they are sexually objectified.

Domestic violence is also a reflection, in part, of male preroga-tive in the public space. If they represent the household in whatever kind of community or public space exists, men also sustain the pre-rogative to discipline those within. The household is itself a "little kingdom," according to colloquial and legal habits of mind. While women may be thought to have moral influence in the household, men are assumed to have disciplinary and juridical power. In the US, physical violence in the household has been rendered criminal only since the 1970s, named as "domestic violence." Before then, violence among those in intimate relationships of any sort—whether familial or dating—was considered a private affair, to be worked out within the private spaces of the family or extended kin/commu-nity network. Sexualized violence and abuse in the family space are now generally actionable in criminal courts as a harm the state must take responsibility for adjudicating.

Feminists have made many different arguments about privacy and masculinist prerogative in the private space. Some have said that the nuclear family is empirically shown to be a space of threat for vulnerable members and therefore should be taken off its pedes-tal as foundational to individual wellbeing, community stability, and, in some narratives, "civilization" itself. In fact, it has been argued, the "family" is more psychically and physically dangerous for individuals—particularly children and women—than the streets or the workplace. Black feminists, however, point to the fact that Black people in the US have never had the same "right" to the pri-vate familial space; Black families have never been placed on ped-estals by culture at large.[23] The legacy of slavery hangs on in the persistent interventions by the state in Black families' lives (e.g., as mentioned above with respect to the hyper-enforcement of child protective services) and the vastly disproportionate levels of incar-ceration of Black fathers and mothers. The heteronormative nuclear family, isolated from extended familial networks, is also unique to middle-class white communities in wealthier liberal countries.

While masculinist sexual violence exists everywhere, its mean-ing and approaches to adjudication will be particular to the context. As discussed in the next section, Black feminists in the US recog-nize the sexualized violence Black women are subjected to in fam-ilies, on the streets, and in institutions, and have led movements that seek alternatives to the criminal legal system for the prevention and adjudication of sexualized harms. We will discuss the creative activist alternatives to criminal legal systems for changing cultures that normalize sexual violence.

Beyond questions about public and private power in the context of the family and intimate violence and abuse, feminists have been deeply divided as to how best to draw lines around what causes and constitutes "sexual violence." I focus here on how this conflict has developed in the US because it has transitioned over the decades into what we currently see as serious differences among feminists worldwide about our relationship to the carceral state.

Some feminists argue that pornography, selling sex, sex harassment, and sexual abuse, including rape, are all effects of male sexual dominance and are forms of sexual violence. Pornography is identified by some feminists as violence against women or individuals objectified as feminine figures, not just in the production of it, but in the educative impact it has as to what "sex" is; "Pornography is the theory, rape is the practice" is a slogan that summarizes this approach. Selling sex, or what is traditionally called "prostitution," perpetuates violence against women or individuals objectified as feminized figures, because women's bodies are considered most valuable when in the service of male desire. That women can make more money stripping or selling sex than they can in most jobs available in the formal economy shows how their personhood is devalued while their bodies are valued only as commodified for sex. Prostitution is inherently coercive, argue some feminists, because no person would sell sex if they had other viable options for making a reasonable living. Further, many individuals who sell sex do so under the coercive terms of a masculinist controlling figure. Few women "choose" to become prostitutes; and even if they do, they face constant threats of violence that will not be recognized because courts will not recognize as a harm sexual violence committed against someone selling sex.

Other feminists have argued that conflating pornography, the selling of sex, sex harassment, and sexual abuse, including rape, constructs male dominance as totalizing and fails to see how women's autonomous desires may include the pornographic, the selling of sex, or even the experience (consensual) of performances of dominance and pain in the context of sex. Women who engage in these activities are not simply pawns of male dominance and are not simply reproducing male forms of desire through enacting violence. Much of the conflict among feminists has been about whether women who produce pornography, even if they call it feminist, or women who engage in selling sex, commonly called "sex workers" in this framing, or women who engage in "male-identified" performances of dominance in same-sex relationships with other women are expressing their desires or reproducing and legitimating male violence and the objectification of others' bodies for sexual satisfaction.

So-called "pro-sex" feminists argue that the value of discovering the full range of women's sexuality is diminished if feminists focus only on the dangers we face as sexual subordinates to men. They argue feminism should not reproduce the inherently conservative ideology that sex should be "safe" from objectification or even commodification, since that in itself reproduces the moral prudishness that has historically controlled and inhibited women's sexuality and the liberatory quality of sexuality generally.

These arguments became so fierce in the US as to be identified as the "sex wars"[24]; but the debate has changed in the 21st century into one embedded in liberal ideology. The "pro-sex" arguments about the liberatory quality of sexuality and differentiated ways of practicing sex (sadomasochism being the most controversial among feminists in the 1980s) have diminished in visibility and/or morphed into arguments about free speech (pornography) or freedom of contract/unionization (sex work). Under the influence of Title IX and other legal means by which sexual harassment and violence have been identified as discriminatory and therefore actionable under civil rights law, the violence against women movement has become institutionalized in the form of trainings about how not to sexually harass or abuse subordinates or colleagues, students, or classmates. A cottage industry of consultants now exists to help companies avoid liability for harassment or abuse carried on by their employees by putting in place trainings and policy directives. The Power and Control Wheel, describing the dynamics of domestic violence, now hangs in police stations and state-funded agencies. The critical edge of the early conflicts among feminists about these issues has been filed down. Many still involved as free speech advocates and anti-violence workers identify as feminists; the activism and policies that are most visible in the public space are identified with the liberal framework I describe throughout this book.

Early in contemporary feminist movements, debates centered on where women's desire or multiple kinds of desire live in the context of institutions defined by men. Since the early 2000s, the conflict among feminists has more explicitly focused on whether and how the movement against violence against women has been complicit with the explosive growth, since the 1980s, in the law enforcement arm of the state and the criminal legal system.

FEMINISMS AND THE CARCERAL STATE

As discussed above, feminists have struggled to bring sexualized violence out of the out of the shadows of stigma and shame; this requires politicization of those gendered and sexed dynamics that normalize sexual violence. Through speak-outs and grassroots organizing of shelters, crisis response, and self-defense training, feminists have brought otherwise personalized and stigmatized experiences of sexual violence into the public space. Early grassroots efforts transformed over time into appeals to state agencies. Adequate funding, time, and space were impossible to sustain, and it became common sense among many advocates and agencies to pressure the state, at all levels of our federal system, to fund and help organize anti-violence efforts. Feminists simultaneously appealed to agencies that provide social welfare (for shelters and support for those experiencing domestic abuse) and to law enforcement agencies, including the police, prosecutors, and courts. Because making law enforcement recognize sexual violence as a serious social harm rather than a personal issue was such a profoundly heavy lift, this area of reform efforts received more attention. The criminal legal system became a central battleground for feminist reformers and activists against sexual violence. In this section, I discuss appeals and struggles within the context of the criminal legal system as they have moved to the forefront of feminist debate over the last 20 years. Self-identified feminist approaches to sexual violence have shifted significantly from grassroots activism—with its emphasis on self-defense/empowerment, the re-education of culture about sex, and protest—to a focus on law enforcement agencies and the criminal courts for compensation for victims and accountability on the part of perpetrators.

This section briefly outlines recent arguments about whether feminists working against sexual violence should go to the criminal legal system for resources and justice. As noted, feminist responses to the scourge of sexual and domestic violence have taken many forms. In many communities globally, the movement against rape and domestic violence has been driven by a grassroots militancy, with women and girls supporting one another through opening shelters, publicly naming and shaming alleged rapists and abusers, and developing self-defense and empowerment strategies. Speak-outs and street protests upend discursive regimes that frame the issue in terms of individual moral failings on the part of perpetrators and victims. Shifting attention from the perpetrator's or victim's individual motives, identity, or status to the structural and cultural terms on which gender and race work to make sexual violence a constant threat and reality has—albeit unevenly across time and space—created new possibilities for ending sexual violence. However, while sexualized and gendered forms of harassment, violence and sexual assault are politicized by these strategies, engagement with systems of law enforcement and criminal legal processes has taken the movement down a path of demanding protection rather than autonomy and freedom and identified longer periods of punishment by incarceration as the measure of justice.

This discussion focuses primarily on US policy and practices with respect to the criminalization of domestic abuse and sexual assault. The US has the highest per-capita incarceration rate in the world. Given the efforts to criminalize sexual violence (render it a public harm, not a personal issue), feminisms in the US grapple with complicity with a deeply flawed and unjust criminal legal system. While the relationship between feminist efforts against sexual violence and the criminal legal system have always been fraught, the issue of whether feminists working against sexual violence should engage at all with law enforcement agencies has come to the forefront of debates.

To get at the issues at hand, we can look at a significant policy shift at the federal level about which feminists disagree. In the US, the Violence Against Women Act (VAWA) was first passed in 1994 and has been revised/renewed on a five-year schedule since. This act was the first federal funding directly addressed to domestic abuse and sexual assault. VAWA was one small part of an Omnibus Crime Bill (OCB) supported by a bipartisan majority in Congress and signed by a Democratic president. The OCB drastically increased federal penalties for drug crimes, applied the death penalty to 60 additional crimes, and dramatically boosted federal funding for policing agencies and expansion of state and federal prison systems. It contributed significantly to the militarization and of police forces, funding for prosecutorial resources, and prison building. The general consensus among scholars and activists is that the OCB facilitated the US having by far the highest rate of incarceration in the world. That VAWA was part of this particular bill and that many self-identified feminists supported and continue to support it have led to intensive discussions among feminists as to whether engagement with the criminal legal system will diminish levels of sexual violence and provide care and, ultimately, justice for those victimized. Feminist critics of the criminal legal system seek alternative means to stopping sexual violence and holding those who commit acts of sexual violence accountable.

By 1994, the feminist rape law reform movement had advanced rape shield laws, challenged marital exemptions for rape accusations, expanded the definition of "rape" beyond "forcible intercourse," and sensitized judges and juries to the treatment of alleged victims as witnesses. Domestic abuse had been written into state codes as a criminal offense and police were being trained to understand abuse in the home as a criminal offense rather than a personal issue. In relative terms, VAWA enhanced these efforts through funding for the training of law enforcement workers and victim assistance programs in prosecutors' offices. It also offered grants to social service (the "welfare" side) agencies, shelters, and programs. The disparity in funding—law enforcement agencies are allotted 30 times the dollars reserved for service agencies—shows that priorities among those supporting VAWA continue to prioritize policing, prosecution, and incarceration as solutions to sexualized violence.

Since the early 21st century, with the growth of the Black Lives Matters movement, the creation of innocence projects that have led to the exoneration of thousands of incarcerated individuals, organized opposition to mandatory prison sentences, and challenges to catastrophic overcrowding in prisons, we have seen the emergence of powerful police and prison reform and abolition efforts. Anticarceral activism and critical studies of the war on drugs and mass incarceration such as the massively influential *The New Jim Crow: Mass Incarceration in the Age of Colorblindness* by Michelle Alexander have engaged feminists in a radical rethinking of support for federal legislation like VAWA and, regionally and locally, our focus on the criminal legal system as a site through which to end sexual violence or remedy its effects.[25] Black feminists have driven the critique of mainstream feminist solutions that identify the criminal legal system as a resource rather than part of the problem to be solved.

Given the formation of the modern nation-state as a masculinist project, feminists think deeply and critically about the politics, ethics, and efficacy of state-funded and organized reforms and whether they serve our ends of gender justice. In the case of feminist efforts against sexual violence, despite reforms in federal and state laws and courtroom procedures, rape and sexual abuse remain some of the most underreported and, if reported, under-policed and under-prosecuted behaviors identified as criminal. While convictions for sex crimes like child pornography have increased dramatically in the 21st century,[26] the credibility of those claiming sexual abuse—from boys and girls in athletics to women in the entertainment industry to waged laborers in farm fields and women in college dorms—is persistently undermined by deeply held cultural biases that work against those who are structurally and personally vulnerable and in favor of those with authority and influence. Since 2017, through the global #MeToo movement, millions of people who have experienced sexual abuse have spoken out against those who hold extraordinary cultural and political power and influence; figures like Harvey Weinstein, Larry Nassar, Richard Strauss, and Bill Cosby have finally been exposed as serial abusers of women, girls, and boys. However, we have only to look at how long such serial abusers were allowed to continue their abuse to see that criminalizing sexualized violence, the primary site for social condemnation and punishment of certain acts and behaviors, has not worked to change the masculinist culture that perpetuates (among all genders) sexual violence. Consider further that it requires hundreds of claims before allegations against serial abusers are given credibility. This signifies that individual women, girls, and boys are still not heard as credible when claiming sexual abuse.

In other words, engagement with the carceral state has shifted the discursive framing of sexual violence and forced it to be taken more seriously. However, the carceral state is organized along racialized, classed, and gendered lines which constitute only some victims (young white cis females) as worthy of attention; focuses attention on conservative, moral, and individualized interpretations of sexual violence; and sustains a model of patriarchal protectionism *vis-à-vis* women and children. Engagement with the criminal legal system is now considered part of the problem rather than a solution for many feminists. They have turned their attention from fixing a flawed system that relies on punitive measures to experimenting with and establishing non-state organizational forms that focus on restorative practices that challenge gendered assumptions. Angela Y. Davis is an intellectual leader and activist in the prison abolition movement. Davis wrote *Are Prisons Obsolete* in 2003, deploying class, gender and race arguments to present a discourse of what the world could look like without prisons.[27] She and colleagues Gina Dent, Beth Ritchie, and Erica Meiners published *Abolition. Feminism. Now,*[28] which develops feminist prison abolitionism as a movement to create different means to do justice that will undermine the traditional retributive and punitive habits we otherwise cannot see past. It argues that prison abolitionism and feminisms overlap insofar as care is a central theme. Using community-inspired care as a touchstone for feminism rather than punishment as a sign of how or whether we care about sexualized victimization will potentially build a world that does not rely on prisons to serve justice.

This approach resists measuring progress in terms of arrests, prosecutions, convictions, and lengths of sentences. Rather, we should think about and act on political transformations of gendered, raced, and classed existence, radically shifting norms that condition the possibility of sexual violence in the many varied forms it takes. While it can guard against harmful behavior, the deterrent quality of law has little impact on rates of sexually abusive behavior. Law shapes political norms, but it is primarily reactive in practice. Affirmation of the harm is crucial and criminal legal proceedings can occasionally satisfy that basic requirement of justice. However, proactive political organizing is necessary to radically change the terms on how masculinity, in its performances and because of its prerogatives, persists in its most aggressive and violent forms.

Feminist prison abolitionism focuses on eliminating the terms on which sexual violence is normalized rather than finding our way to justice after the fact. This strategy does not preclude the deployment of law to change attitudes about and outcomes of sexual violence, but it does take into account the inherent limits of law as a site of social change. It is by undoing patriarchy, not relying on patriarchal institutions, that gendered and sexual relationships will change and sexual violence will become literally unthinkable.

FEMINISM AND "WOMEN-ONLY" SPACES: TRANSGENDER POLITICS

People who do not identify with the male or female sex/gender assigned to them at birth have always existed everywhere. "Transgender" is the way people who experience this dissonance at any time in their life refer to themselves. As Judith Butler, among others, has argued, the announcement "It's a boy" or "It's a girl" is an act of calling into gendered being the figure pictured on an ultrasound screen or the baby newly birthed.[29] This is a moment when sex is "assigned." There are no tests done; it is the appearance of genitalia that results in this announcement or assignment—or, as some would have it, determination—of sex. Infants whose genitalia is less defined or "indeterminate" as one or the other of the binary girl/boy will be identified as requiring special treatment of some sort. "Difficult decisions" will have to be made about surgical intervention or which sex the parents will choose to raise the child into.

The act of assigning sex tells us that while biology plays a significant role in how we are gendered, social existence, habits, presumptions, and social norms condition our gendered existence. Calling someone a girl or a boy because they have a vagina or a penis is a decision—one that most human beings, unconsciously committed to a certain way of regulating gender identity, make when a baby is born. This indicates that this decision, repeated over and over until it seems like a girl or a boy was just there waiting to be identified, genders us. There is nothing necessary about the attachment of "girl" and "boy" to one version of anatomy or the other. Hormones matter a lot; no transgender advocate would say otherwise, as hormone therapy is often necessary to help transgender individuals feel in a physiological way like the gender—whether male, female, or otherwise—they really are. No transgender advocate would say biology is unimportant. However, biology, including the shape of genitalia or chromosomal mixes at birth, does not in any simple way make a person a girl or a boy. Many individuals can produce massive levels of testosterone and have "normal" male genitalia and identify as women. Likewise, estrogen and a vagina can be biological facts a person lives with, but that person may really be a man. Some who experience this require changes to the biological facts of their bodies to correct their gender identity. Others may feel comfortable in their body without surgery, enacting the gender they are by way of gender expression, style, or appearance. Those who do not feel or experience themselves to be either girl or boy or woman or man may identify as non-binary and express their sense of self by way of style, appearance, surgery, or comportment.

Transgender people, who have in common a dissonance between the sex assigned at birth and how they feel and experience themselves as gendered beings, have been identifying and struggling for rights and recognition with feminist and queer movements for decades. Many feminists are transgender and/or queer. However, since the publication of Janice Raymond's book *Transsexual Empire*[30] and the response by Sandy Stone,[31] the "question" of whether there exists a feminism that includes transwomen has raged on paper, in activist groups, and now among those striving to influence mainstream policymaking.

WOMEN-IDENTIFIED? OR WOMEN-ONLY?

This discussion is included in this chapter because some feminists and advocates for transgender rights and recognition have been deeply at odds over policies. While the fight has been ongoing among self-identified feminist communities for decades, it has since the early 2010s been mainstreamed as right-wing, anti-feminist groups have opportunistically attached themselves to the question of "women's rights" in campaigns to demonize and dehumanize transgender people. It is a policy question because spaces are being identified—in particular, public bathrooms and athletics teams—by elected officials and legislated as "women-only" in the sense that only women identified as such at birth may enter. This is being done in the name of protecting and respecting women with little acknowledgment that it is those assigned male at birth who remain men who commit the sexualized harms against women—those assigned at birth *and* transgender men and women. "Women-only" spaces have been assumed to be identifiable by many feminists since the early days of consciousness-raising and separatist elements of the feminist movement. Those radical women-identified women spaces are not what right-wing commentators are referring to when they discuss "women's right to safety from male predators." However, those kinds of spaces, created and cultivated as political spaces of resistance to patriarchal dominance primarily by self-identified radical lesbian feminists, are a precursor to the much more public fights happening now about "women-only spaces" like public bathrooms and athletics teams.

Further, these gender-based identity clashes have mainstream histories beyond what is happening among feminists and feminisms in the 21st century. For example, the gender segregated public bathroom dates to the slow entry to women into public spaces at the turn of the 20th century. The Victorian culture struggled with how women, always conceived of as sexually vulnerable, could possibly do such intimate things like use the toilet when outside the home. It was a patriarchal and protectionist policy to segregate bathrooms even when those spaces had enclosed stalls. This book is about feminisms as such, and how that term is being taken up differently by many different kinds of feminists, gathering meanings and changing policies and lives around the globe. However, as I hope is clear throughout this book, it is always worth questioning whether a particular position identified as feminist may be colluding with patriarchal ideologies of protectionism, separate spheres, or theological/naturalized versions of what it means to be male or female that hold in place the hierarchy of male/female, masculine/feminine, man/woman. Within the spaces of contemporary public battles over "women-only" spaces feminisms are yet again shifting in terms of principle and strategy how they articulate feminist policy positions.

Feminists have been supporting and contesting the category of "women-only spaces," not in the name of protecting women's virtue, but—especially since the late 1960s—in the name of making space for women to find their voices, theorize their condition, and act specifically as women, as a class in solidarity with other women. I take a brief look here at a very different kind of space described by its feminist founders and creators as women-only. I do this to point out that self-identified feminists themselves do not agree about the category "woman" and how our interpretations and enactments of the naturalized binaries of male/female or masculine/feminine serve the end of autonomy and/or justice.

The Michigan Womyn's Festival, over time, became the quintessential lesbian-feminist space. It was founded by sisters Lisa and Kristie Vogel and their friend Mary Kindig. It was to be a woman-only, lesbian-feminist identified Woodstock (referencing the famous music festival of 1969). It was, from the beginning, associated with a particular feminism—a separatist feminism that argues women are freer to be their authentic selves when out of the company of men. It identified itself not as anti-male but as pro-woman. The festival happened annually for a remarkable 40 years, until 2015. It was located on 250 acres of forested land in Michigan and included workshops, collective meals, camping, music, many kinds of stage performances, and a woman-identified marketplace where women could sell their creations and services. Numbers of attendees ran from 3,000 to 10,000 over the years. It lasted for a week—long enough to become like a woman-only city run on feminist principles, with directors who oversaw the festival each year, a volunteer requirement for all participants, and organized governing intentions (Vogel's word for what otherwise might be called "guidelines").

One of those intentions of governance was to disallow the open presence of transwomen at the festival. How this intention was carried out in practice has been debated since 1991, when a transwoman was expelled from the festival. This event inspired the organization of a protest encampment, Camp Trans, down the road from MichFest. The views of organizers on the participation of transwomen are not clear, but some sources summarize them as "Don't ask, don't tell"—a reference to military policy about gay men and women in the 1990s. Gay men and women could enlist in the military as long as they made no reference to and did not act on their "status" as gay. In the case of MichFest, this was not sufficient, and indeed was insulting, for the transwomen who wished to be a part. The "trans" in transwomen is their identity even while the claim to *be* a woman and to desire recognition as such is also a part. In *Transgressive: A Transwoman on Gender, Feminism, and*

Politics, Rachel Ann Williams describes the inherent danger in a transmisogynist world in which she knows she is a woman no matter if she has masculine characteristics (in her case, a male-like voice), but passing becomes a matter of survival because transphobia inspires violence.[32] Making their presence at MichFest acceptable only if they were "successfully passing" as women made this a dangerous space that reflected the oppressive gendered values of the patriarchal world MichFest claimed to defy. If lesbians were out and safe as women at MichFest, it would make sense that transwomen should be out and safe as women at MichFest.

The trans exclusionary governing principle at MichFest can be contrasted and compared to the mainstream fights about "women-only" spaces and activities, public bathrooms, and athletics teams that emerged in the mid-2010s.

ABOUT PUBLIC BATHROOMS

As mentioned above, gender-segregated public bathrooms were an afterthought in response, in Western cultures, to white, middle-class women entering public spaces in higher numbers. However, women's bathrooms were not built to accommodate the typically longer amount of time necessary to use the toilet, and they tended to be built further away from whatever action was happening in the public space. Equality-minded feminists have argued for more women's bathrooms built in reasonable proximity to the center of activity. This has never been a particularly visible struggle. It was not until 2011 that women's bathrooms were built near enough to the chamber where the Congress met in the Capital building in Washington DC that women representatives would have time to leave and get back in time for a roll-call vote. In 2013, the size of the bathroom was doubled to accommodate increasing numbers of women in Congress.

Women's access to public bathrooms where they could have privacy, specifically from men, has thus been on the agenda of equality-minded feminists. With the increasing visibility of organized transgender movements in the last 20 years, they have come to the attention of right-wing policymakers. Policy surrounding the public women's bathroom has become increasingly fraught. It is matched only by the pitched arguments about trans girls and women participating in female athletics. In 2024, 13 years after the women's bathroom was created in the halls of Congress, Sarah McBride of Delaware—the first transgender woman to be elected to the House of Representatives—was forbidden from using it by the Speaker of the House, Mike Johnson. While transgender people have been using the bathroom for over a decade with no attention being paid, a member of the Republican House caucus brought a resolution forward to make the bathroom only for women assigned female at birth. So-called "bathroom bills" have passed prohibiting transgender people from using the bathroom associated with their lived gender, requiring them to use "single-use" bathrooms or those of the gender they were assigned at birth.

However, following in the spirit of this book, we can read this visible, national "controversy" as generating new and unexpected political possibilities. Conflicts among feminists have material consequences. These arguments inspire or anger those involved and the policies that emerge help or hurt those impacted in very concrete ways. Not being able to use a public bathroom without scrutiny and potential insult or violence or not being allowed to play a sport with the gender with which one identifies inspires justifiable rage. With these very public struggles, the categories of "women" and "woman" and, by virtue of how dualisms or binaries work, "men" and "man" are contested in real life, not just in postmodern theorizing.

I focus here on these policy conflicts, relating them back to the conflict over MichFest because similarly, the fight is over the meaning of "women-only spaces"—or to be more precise, about how feminists think about the category "woman." Feminists who wish to sustain the category as defined by assignment at birth or general anatomical difference from male bodies self-identify as "gender critical." They are identified as "trans-exclusionary radical feminists" since not all self-identified radical feminists are opposed to trans inclusion. Critical analysis of the differences "gender-critical" feminists and trans-positive feminists have over inclusion of trans-women illuminates issues feminists have already raised for decades about essentializing gendered categories of being and experience.

For example, at MichFest, the status of those attending was identified as "womyn-born-womyn" (wby). Yet most feminists have no disagreement with Simone de Beauvoir's classic statement that "One is not born but becomes a woman."[33] MichFest organizers used wbw to describe the status of those welcomed because they are women who had to grow up as women without enjoying the "privileges" of being male/masculine. Yet they used a phrase used by conservatives committed to sustaining a binary/heteronormative system of gender, one that attributes the essential truth of one's gender back to the moment of birth when one is arbitrarily assigned a gender of girl or boy. It did not matter that transwomen may experience themselves as girls in early childhood and suffer the consequences of that difference. One may never "enjoy the privileges" of being male if one is trans. Or, as Rachel Williams states, even if one experiences a shift later in life from being comfortable in a male body and masculine lifestyle to being uncomfortable, it is hardly a simple "choice" to transition either in one's gender expression or in one's body.[34] One feels no less a woman because one is 40 rather than pre-pubescent and "male privilege" is harshly denied when a person comes out as trans. Williams identifies this as transmisogyny.

In most cases, when the status of transwomen is in question, it is the moment of assignment at birth that speaks truth for some; yet that assignment (as Sarah Ahmed discusses—see Chapter 4) is arbitrary and unnecessary. Gender uncertainty messes with us as identifying the gender of an interlocutor conditions relationships, but it need not. Feminists engaging with trans theory and issues argue that the fight about including transwomen in women-only spaces distracts from the work feminists have always done to challenge masculinist dominance and violence against women. If cisgendered women are afraid of men pretending to be women in order to get access and perpetrate harm or to beat them in games, their problem is with cisgendered men, not with transwomen. Thus, they argue the outrage about transwomen coming into "women-only spaces" is driven by moral panic, not by actual experience.

The question of policy around athletics is difficult because bodies are different according to the hormones we associate with male bodies and those we associate with female bodies. However, perhaps the feminist response is to say, "Let us do away with traditional forms of gender segregation in sports." A conversation is starting about co-ed sports—in part, because in reality it is size, strength, and training that condition competitiveness in sport, not merely hormones or biology. We can generalize that "men" are bigger, taller, and have more upper body strength; but this does not apply to all males and, perhaps more importantly, there are different ways of playing—even football and rugby, the quintessentially male-identified games—that do not privilege height, strength, or body mass. In other words, gender-segregated teams in athletics are a choice, not a necessity for the quality or competitiveness of the game. These conversations are being driven not only by individual women who are playing on male-identified sporting teams, but by emergent awareness of the impossibility of making a universalizable and just policy that determines whether a person is a man or a woman in order to place them on one side or the other. These debates could ultimately generate a world in which the binary of male/female as mapped onto masculine/feminine is no longer the basis for identifying who is what. Feminists have longed for this world to de-fang patriarchy. Coming to terms with the current struggles about where transwomen are "allowed" to enter could—if we sustain a critical perspective and avoid falling into the trap of protectionism inspired by the idea of "women-only" spaces—contribute to undoing patriarchal dominance. Marquis Bey names trans feminism as ". . . an assault on the genre of the [hierarchized] binary, that ontological caste that universalizes itself and structures how we are made possible."[35]

Feminisms rightly (re)value and argue in the name of those who identify and are identified as women and girls. Circling the wagons around the category of wbw and attributing trans identities to a desire to take over otherwise female spaces is akin to a moral panic. The phrase "moral panic" was derived from research by Stuart Cohen in the 1960s.[36] It is not an organized effort to demonize an activity or a group. It is rather a response to a generalized and very real sense of crisis in capitalist conditions of existence—and, we could argue in the case of transwomen, a response to a crisis of masculinity magnified by the increasing presence of women and transwomen in public life. Rather than connecting trans politics to the feminist demands to radically reorganize gendered life, transwomen are vilified by some feminists and deployed in the culture wars as (re)constructed males and therefore as necessarily predatory.[37]

As this book shows, feminists have disagreements over ideas and policies that have serious lived consequences for persons of all genders. The fight over women-only spaces has devolved into righteous battles over who can claim the mantle of girl or woman. This is not a fight that will be "won or lost." It does, however, magnify the argument many feminists have been making about the mutability of the category "woman." Lesbian-feminist Monique Wittig famously declared "lesbians" are not women.[38] She claimed this because "woman" is a category necessarily attached to and defined by relationships to male figures. If lesbians refuse this attachment, as suggested earlier in this book, they are also defying the rules of gender that make people into men and women. Not all lesbians understand themselves this way, but it is arguably an outcome of women refusing relationships with men and giving their life energies to women. Homophobia is a reaction of fear about women removing themselves from patriarchal control and about gay men refusing traditional versions of masculinity that rely upon dominant if unspoken cultural agreements about what it feels and looks like.

Taking the argument in a slightly different direction, women who have been the "first" to become lawyers or actors or doctors or elected officials have also "violated" the terms of what it is to be a "woman" and made more space for people called women to take up public roles. Finally, women of color have been marked as "other" than "true women." The politics of respectability which scholar Brittney Cooper writes about (see Chapter 5) is an effort to navigate how Black women in particular can thrive in a world that never understood Black women as deserving dignity and autonomy.

In short, feminists have always challenged the category of "woman." The trans exclusionary position makes no sense in this context. "Woman" as a discursive and lived category of experience is part of the problem feminism has set out to solve in the name of gender justice and freedom. To claim transwomen are intruders rather than women challenging—as feminists have always done—the binary categories, roles, and values patriarchy puts in place is not feminist.

Further, Julia Serrano argues to reclaim rather than criticize the powers of femininity, which she says bring joy, ease, and lightness. She says her suffering as a transwoman was brought on more by anti-feminine misogyny rather than anti-trans sentiments. Transwomen sometimes celebrate the femininity, style, and expression that are stereotypically expected of those identified as women that cisgender women reject. Transwomen also insist they are "women" as such, not non-binary or different from what it is that patriarchy created as the man/woman dualism. This means some transwomen identify as conservative, not feminist, in their desire to live, not just pass, as "real women." Nonetheless, just as the lesbian figuratively challenges masculinist assumptions about female desire, transwomen challenge assumptions about the fixity otherwise assumed between the appearance of genitalia and levels of hormones and gender identity. "Gender-critical" feminists argue this undermines the struggles of women as women because someone who became a woman last year cannot compare herself to a woman who has been such for 50 years. It is this very discussion and the arguments that emerge that keep feminism thinking critically about the categories of "women," "woman," "male/female," and "masculine/feminine." Feminists engage deeply and intensely in these disagreements about categories that define our deepest senses of self; and while outcomes are often painful and unpredictable, if we do not succumb to moral panic, new possibilities emerge.

NOTES

1 Ahmed, Sara, *Living a Feminist Life* (Duke University Press, 2017).

2 Hawkesworth, Mary, "Policy Studies within a Feminist Frame" in *Policy Sciences* vol. 27 (1994) 97–118.

3 Fox, Jennifer and Richard Fox, *Women, Men and US Politics* (Norton Press, 2017).

4 Foster, Emma, "Ecofeminism Revisited: Critical Insights on Contemporary Environmental Governance" in *Feminist Theory* vol. 22 2 (2012) 190–205.

5 Climate One, "Vandana Shiva and the Hubris of Manipulating Nature," July 30, 2021. https://www.climateone.org/audio/vandana-shiva-and-hubris-manipulating-nature

6 Ebron, Paulla and Anna Tsing "Feminism and the Anthropocene: Assessing the Field Through Recent Books" in *Feminist Studies* vol. 43 3 (2017) 658–683.

7 USAID, a development agency founded in 1961, shifted focus to gender equality in the 1980s in light of data that shows women's work is severely undervalued and under-supported. Research shows how much more is accomplished when women, rather than men, are given development resources. This editorial was published before USAID was eliminated by the Trump administration in 2025, in part because of references to equality, gender, and empowerment in its project statements. Voice of America, "Supporting Women's Economic Participation," January 17, 2025. https://editorials.voa.gov/a/supporting-women-s-economic-participation/7940522.html. (Note that the Voice of America, the publisher of this editorial, has also been shut down.)

8 *Morris v. Commissioner of Internal Revenue*, 697 F.3d 568 7th Circuit (2012).

9 *Dothard v. Rawlinson*, 433 U.S. 321 (1977).

10 *Meritor Savings Bank v. Vinson*, 477 U.S. 57 (1986).

11 *Harris v. Forklift Systems, Inc.*, 510 U.S. 17 (1993).

12 *Oncale v. Sundowner Offshore Services, Inc.*, 523 U.S. 75 (1998).

13 The Inter-Parliamentary Union (IPU) was founded in 1989 in Geneva as a forum through which parliamentary governments from across the globe promote democracy. It published a study of 55 women-identified members of parliament from around the world and established through interviews and contextual research that women parliamentarians experience high levels of sexual harassment and assault. IPU, "IPU Study Reveals Widespread Sexism, Harassment and Violence against Women MPs," October 26, 2016. https://www.ipu.org/news/press-releases/2016-10/ipu-study-reveals-widespread-sexism-harassment-and-violence-against-women-mps

14 Kanougiya, Shristi, Muthusamy Sivakami, Nayreen Daruwalla, David Osrin, et al, "Prevalence, Pattern, and Predictors of Formal Help-Seeking for Intimate Partner Violence against Women: Findings from India's Cross-Sectional National Family Health Surveys 3 (2005–2006) and 4 (2015–2016)" in *BMC Public Health* vol. 22 2386 (2022).

15 As quoted in Cavallero, Luci et al. "Argentina's Anti-Capitalist Feminism," *Jacobin Magazine*, February 9, 2018. https://jacobin.com/2018/09/argentinas-anticapitalist-feminism

16 In this section, though much of the literature I reference identifies those who can get pregnant as "women" and "girls," I will use gender-neutral terms. The inclusion of trans and non-binary individuals is crucial to thinking about reproductive justice. Transmen and non-binary people do get pregnant and seek reproductive care.

17 [Endnote Data is Missing]

18 Roberts, Dorothy, *Killing the Black Body* (Vintage Press, 1997).

19 Guttmacher Institute, "Unintended Pregnancy and Abortion Worldwide." Fact Sheet, March 2022. https://www.guttmacher.org/fact-sheet/induced-abortion-worldwide.

20 SisterSong, "Reproductive Justice." https://www.sistersong.net/reproductive-justice/

21 MacKinnon, Catharine, *Feminism Unmodified* (Harvard University Press, 1988).

22 Erikson, Josephina and Cecilia Josefsson, "Equal Playing Field? On the Intersection between Gender and Being Young in the Swedish Parliament" in *Politics, Groups and Identities* vol. 9 2 (2019) 1–20.

23 Collins, Patricia Hill, *Black Sexual Politics* (Routledge Press, 2004).

24 Ferguson, Ann, "Sex War: The Debate between Libertarian and Radical Feminists" in *Signs* vol. 10 1 (1984) 106–112.

25 Alexander, Michelle, *The New Jim Crow: Mass Incarceration in the Age of Color Blindness* (New Press, 2010).

26 Bernstein, Elisabeth, "The Sexual Politics of the New Abolitionism" in *Differences* vol. 18 5 (2007) 128–151.

27 Davis, Angela, *Are Prisons Obsolete?* (Seven Stories Press, 2003).

28 Davis, Angela, Gina Dent, Erica Meiers and Beth Ritchie, *Abolition. Feminism. Now.* (Haymarket Books, 2022).

29 Butler, Judith, *Gender Trouble* (Routledge, 1990).

30 Raymond, Janice, *The Transsexual Empire: The Making of the She-Male* (Beacon Press, 1979).

31 Stone, Sandy, *The* Empire *Strikes Back: A Posttransexual Manifesto* (Advanced Communication Technology Laboratory, Department of Radio and Television, University of Texas at Austin, 1987). https://sandystone.com/empire-strikes-back.pdf

32 Williams, Rachel Ann, *Transgressive: A Transwoman on Gender, Feminism, and Politics* (Jessica Kingsley Press, 2019).

33 Beauvoir, Simone de *The Second Sex*, trans. Constance Borde and Sheila Malovany-Chevallier (Vintage Books, 2011), 283.

34 Williams, ibid. 52.

35 Bey, Marquis, *Black Trans Feminism* (Duke University Press, 2022) 5.

36 Cohen, Stanley, *Folk Devils and Moral Panics: The Creation of the Mods and Rockers* (MacGibbon and Kee, 1972).

37 Raymond, Janice G., *The Transsexual Empire: The Making of the She-Male* (Beacon Press, 1979).

38 Wittig, Monique, *The Straight Mind and Other Essays* (Beacon Press, 1992).

4

THE PERSONAL IS POLITICAL

INTRODUCTION

In *Tied up in Iran: Women, Social Change, and the Politics of Everyday Life in post-Revolutionary Iran* Claire Moruzzi offers an interpretation of "the personal is political."[1] She introduces her book with a discussion of "Two Women," an Iranian film about women students of architecture and the closing down of possibilities after the revolution of 1979. She compares her interpretation of the film to that of Iranian women with whom she discussed the film. She first concludes that this film portrays an Iranian woman's helplessness and passivity in the face of male violence as the theocratic state cracks down on women's autonomy and freedoms. Upon discussion with Iranian friends, however, she concludes the film represents not that woman's particular status as a victim of men, but the betrayal experienced in the post-revolutionary (1979) context when the nationalist project was built on women's backs. The helplessness and passivity were not a representation of stereotypical responses of women to abuse; rather, they were a lived reality in the context of the revolutionary shifts from being relatively autonomous as individuals to being deployed as pawns of the theological patriarchy.

Moruzzi suggests that in the reformist 1990s, Iranian women were "trying to catch up" with what they had missed since the revolution; the film captures this desire in its complexity as it shapes women's lives. In other words, she reads the phrase as telling us that every woman's life is personal and particular but is also a prism of the national experience. Moruzzi suggests that the personal is

DOI: 10.4324/9781003264682-4

political because the political can be read off the apparently individualized and personal experiences of women. Hers is a generative and constructive approach to interpreting the phrase discussed in this chapter: "the personal is political."

There are innumerable references to and discussions of this phrase in theoretical, activist, and even fictional feminist writing from the last 60 years. It is associated with second-wave feminism, but no single political movement or theory can lay claim to its meaning. This chapter identifies several contexts in which it appears and some of the meaning(s) it has accrued over time. Identity politics, debates about experience and authenticity, and critical reframings of the public and the private refer to this apparently simple catchphrase. Its influence and fluctuating meanings are inscribed in the history of new social movements and newer counter-publics.[2] Some argue it has inspired a "personalized" politics in a way that breeds disunity and fractured sensibilities about the functions and effects of institutionalized and structural injustices and inequalities. A more optimistic evaluation, however, is that it authorizes a radically expanded space for politicized and politicizing reflection on the part of the subject/citizen, and more capacious interpretive frameworks for challenging illegitimate forms of power and dominance. This reflects how Moruzzi's interpretation of the otherwise apparently personal stories of the two women in the 1999 film can be read to reflect the revolutionary national/political effects of the 1979 revolution.

HISTORICAL EMERGENCE

Second-wave feminism was not the first or only 20th century social movement to invoke the spirit of the phrase "the personal is political." Feminism did, however, introduce it into the popular lexicon and it became a crucial, albeit deeply and sometimes fiercely contested, reference point for feminist politics. I therefore begin with a brief account of the experiences and thinking of women who planted the seeds of the second wave of feminist politics in the US.

Sara Evans' history of white Southern women's experiences in the civil rights movement through the 1960s traces the journey of the phrase "the personal is political" into second-wave feminist discourse and activism.[3] Her work focuses particularly on women as organizers in the Student Non-Violent Coordinating Committee

(SNCC) and then in the Southern Student's Organizing Committee (SSOC).[4] "The personal is political" resonated deeply with women who, through their political organizing experiences in the civil rights movement, became painfully aware of how their daily activities and personal lives were shaped by unstated assumptions about male superiority and prerogative.

Evans describes young civil rights activists as creating a way of life as much as a set of ideas. They ate, slept, had sex, formed intimate relationships, and worked in very close proximity with, and often under threat in, hostile neighborhoods and rural communities. The movement was their life.[5] Early SNCC organizers were committed to enacting, not just invoking, what was called the "beloved community" by Martin Luther King and non-violent social justice activists. The organizing environment itself was thus intensely personal and political; activists aspired to enact a model of the egalitarian and democratic world in which they wanted to live. The "beloved community" invoked ethical claims, calling upon activists to create relationships of solidarity that go beyond the abstract unity inspired by shared analysis or leadership based on traditional rhetorical skills or the intellectual mastery of issues.

This commitment did not ultimately create expanding or longterm political unity. Rather, it became a generative space of sometimes harsh and painful conflict that would, over the long term, inform understanding of the significance of sex and sexism as they entwined with race and racism among women and men in both the SNCC and the SSOC. Many who were involved in the organization of the civil rights movement would ultimately become involved in radically differentiated political movements—Black nationalism, second-wave feminism, and a reinvigorated Students for a Democratic Society among them. The differentiated social movements that emerged from the civil rights and student movements of the 1960s would reflect variations on the theme of the personal being political.

In the environment of civil rights organizing, where the personal was inevitably politicized in an immediate sense, white women were often assigned or assumed to be responsible for traditionally female tasks such as housekeeping, filing or organizing the office, typing the press releases rather than writing them, and making the coffee. And the presence of white women in the movement was imbued with racial and sexual significance. White women could not travel to most communities with Black men and sex between Black men and white women in the movement was fraught, associated as it was with a challenge to white masculinity and with the standing threat from white men to torture and murder Black men, especially those who appeared to associate with white women for any reason. Unlike their white male companions, white women organizers had to challenge roles forced upon them by political friends and enemies alike. They contended with assumptions about female behavior, goals, and responsibilities that were not only a part of the general culture, but—as they recognized with some distress—imbued in their subjectivity. The tenacity of traditional racialized, bourgeois roles for white women kept them in the safer counties, less likely to be registering voters and more likely to be sexualized by men in the movement. Young white women had, of necessity, to forge a new sense of self, to redefine the meaning of being a woman quite apart from the flawed, disempowering images they had inherited.[6]

Black women did not experience the sexualization of relationships in the same way; nor did they experience the protective "chivalry" white women came to despise. Black women's immediate conflicts were often with white women, not men, in the movement. In this sense, the personal was political in that the personal relationships white women formed with Black men were both personal and political to Black women. Those relationships constituted a deeply felt personal affront to some Black women, even while they simultaneously could be interpreted in the context of resistance to miscegenation, one of the most closely held and dangerous of "racial traditions" in the US. Whatever the "truth" of the personal relationships that developed in the SNCC, Black women themselves were alternatively marginalized or reified; ultimately, they were assumed to be detached from such matters. Black women made critical claims about these issues in the moment and, as the feminist movement emerged with a predominantly white cast of visible figures and set of issues predominantly associated with white women's lives, launched critiques of the race-blindness of what became mainstream feminist discourse.[7]

In short, "the personal is political" was enacted in the gendered and sexed dynamics of the civil rights movement, the Black Power movement, and the student movement. "The personal is political" was thus invoked as a challenge within and among those movements to see the limits of their own vision as to what constitutes the "political." It simultaneously signified a quest for authenticity in one's pursuit of justice. In some of its original invocations, the phrase announced the imperative for reflexivity about one's own position of privilege or oppression in any given context. It called for avoiding the imposition of one's values on others as a means to create a participatory democracy. And finally, it indicated that each person has at least a thread of their identity ensnared in oppressive relationships; that no one can claim to be "free" from alienation or oppression as a subject or as an objectified other. The organizing principle of new social movements, "look to one's own oppression," called for self-reflection that would lead to revelations of complicity with or victimization by oppressive relationships on the part of each individual. Ultimately, "the personal is political" would inspire women to insist that what had been thought of as, alternatively, moral issues (sex) or trivial offenses (sexism) in everyday interactions were symptoms of oppressive norms and structural forces.

"THE PERSONAL IS POLITICAL" AND THE SECOND WAVE OF FEMINISM

In 1965, Casey Hayden and Mary King—two white women from the South who were deeply embedded in civil rights activism early in the movement—wrote what they called a "kind of memo."[8] Their immediate purpose was to open dialogue, particularly with Black women in the SNCC, about women's place in the organization and in society at large. The language of the personal figures prominently in the memo, both as the "subjective" reason Hayden and King were speaking to the issue of sex caste and because the transformation of the personal was, for movement activists at the time, said to be a path to radical and progressive political transformation:

> Having learned from the movement to think radically about the personal worth and abilities of people whose role in society had gone unchallenged before, a lot of women in the movement have begun trying to apply those lessons to their own relations with men. Each of us probably has her own story of the various results, and of the internal struggle occasioned by trying to break out of very deeply learned fears, needs, and

self-perceptions, and of what happens when we try to replace them with concepts of people and freedom learned from the movement and organizing.[9]

The memo eloquently describes the personalized struggles of women to confront the deeply subjective constraints of femininity. The reference to each woman having her own story of internal struggle as a woman in relationship to men invokes the spirit that would infuse consciousness-raising among radical feminist groups later in the decade.

Hayden and King's memo had little immediate effect. However, it circulated nationally among women in the new left movements and inspired them to organize women's workshop sessions at meetings. Finally, the hostile response by the majority of men at a 1967 meeting of Students for a Democratic Society to a working document produced by the women's liberation workshop inspired women activists to begin to meet altogether independently of the established left organizations. A subsequent meeting of the National Conference for New Politics (NCNP) in Chicago confirmed that women would not see their demands for equality and recognition met in the male-dominated new left movements. Women began to organize independently as women against sex oppression.[10]

Women-only meetings would eventually come to be more formally organized as consciousness-raising groups. Radical feminists, many of whom were formerly deeply involved in the new left, insisted that women's oppression must be seen as independent of and even prior to racial and class oppressions.

Among radical feminists, "the personal is political" became a method and a claim. This occurred in the context of consciousness-raising groups, which became the means to the end of politicizing women's understanding of what they had normally experienced and normatively identified as personal problems. Over a few years, even while consciousness-raising groups proliferated, feminists became skeptical of this method of politicizing otherwise privatized issues; as did Carol Williams Payne when she wrote about her group becoming more like a social club than a political organization, describing consciousness-raising as becoming an end in itself. Jo Freeman famously critiqued the acclaimed "structurelessness" of consciousness-raising groups. She identified the egalitarian method of sharing personal problems to see what individuals in the group had in common as a developmental moment—but one to which participants became too attached. Freeman argued that attempting to sustain a structureless group will always lead to a group with informal structure in the form of elites, friendship groups, and "stars" who are identified not by the group but by the media or outside influences beyond the control of the group. As this occurs, participants begin to take things personally and "the personal is political" takes on an entirely new and negative meaning as destructive and unacknowledged power relationships develop within and around the group.[11] In organizational terms, the personal became political as radical egalitarianism devolved into conflicts over prerogative and visibility. Nonetheless, over time, consciousness-raising became a site of feminist reinventions of the personal and discoveries of systemic oppression related to normative masculinity and femininity. They were places where gender and sex became contested references related to social justice rather than politically neutral roles or activities that existed outside of power relationships.[12]

In the early 1970s, radical feminists organized specifically against sexual violence in the many forms it adopts, including prostitution, pornography, violence against women, sexual assault and rape, and sexual harassment.[13] The damage done by a patriarchal order to the possibilities of women's sexuality became a theory and a political claim that the male use and abuse of women's sexuality are the source of women's oppression. As the movement grew beyond the early small group models of discussion and activism, arrangements and institutions long buried in the space of the "private," constructed on the terms of modern liberalism, were identified as a cause of suffering for women, no matter their background.

Inspired by the necessity to expose the collective harms they discovered in consciousness-raising groups, to raise public consciousness, and to provoke political responses, such as legislation and funding for organizational purposes, radical feminists organized speak-outs. The earliest speak-outs were about abortion rights, organized to highlight the white maleness of the legislative bodies that were deciding the future of women's reproductive lives and the harm done by criminalizing abortion.[14] Speak-outs were initially understood as politicizing the personal because women came into public spaces, the streets, town halls, and Capitol buildings to tell of experiences otherwise obscured by liberalism's romance with the privacy of sex, sexuality, reproduction, and familial relationships and arrangements, no matter how exclusionary, exploitative, abusive, or violent. Speak-outs were organized to show that abuse and violence are not personal aberrations, but rather the norm for millions of women and children (stories of survival of child sexual abuse were also told in these forums). They sought recognition of historical and collective failures to render a just society. This interpretation of the phrase "the personal is political" anticipates public empathy with otherwise individualized suffering obscured by the demands of privacy. The publicizing of the harm constitutes a kind of shaming as a means to inspire fairer and more just responses to otherwise covert violence.

Speak-outs and other public actions ruptured the appearance that all was well in the home, the obstetrician's office, the workplace, or on the streets (barring the stranger or the pathological individual who threatened or "violated" women). Annual "Take Back the Night" speak-outs and marches were organized as assertions of women's right to appear in public, at whatever time of day or in whatever configuration of style and attitude they chose, without being targeted for rape or assaultive speech.[15] Unlike consciousness-raising groups in their ideal form, speak-outs were not about deliberating the significance and meaning of experiences in the interest of building political arguments or creating a deliberative space that could generate political action. Speak-outs publicized sexualized and gendered harms and injustice, showing that they are not about immoral or abnormal behaviors of deviant individuals, but instead about normatively masculinist prerogatives and entitlements. The recognition that otherwise "personal" suffering was not an effect of personal failure or perception, but of relationships of power and dominance, inspired women to argue for reforms in rape law and marital law, and "domestic violence" became a statutory criminal offense. By the late 1980s, it was possible for wives to claim rape by men who were their husbands[16] and for women to claim "sexual harassment" as discrimination rather than flirting in the workplace[17]; and the fact that "stranger rape" was the exception to the rule of sexual assault of women and girls by friends and relatives was no longer dismissed as propaganda against the traditional family or the romance of seduction.[18] In this decade, the personal became political in the sense that personal suffering was made public; subsequently, the personal became a space where society would begin seeing and naming criminal behavior, not just worrying about dysfunctional relationships.

As sexuality came to the forefront of second-wave feminist concerns, like earlier commitments to radical egalitarianism, it was generative of conflict. By the 1980s, sexuality had become one of the most contested areas among feminists, to the point where that era is identified as the era of the "sex wars."[19] Feminists were torn about whether to focus only on the dangers of sex and sexuality and the material facts of male and masculinist dominance, coercion, and physical violence; or to simultaneously elaborate the pleasures of sex and sexuality as potentially liberatory, and thus political, whether enacted with men or women, monogamously or promiscuously, in private or in public.[20] Either way one turned to understand sexuality, "the personal is political" became ever more salient as the debate itself illustrated that sex and sexuality—traditionally codified in moral terms related to individual desires and behaviors and veiled by liberal commitments to "privacy"—are governed by relationships of power, inequality, and interests.[21]

As the white women Sara Evans and Alice Echols describe were alienated from male-dominated organizations that trivialized or dismissed their presence and participation, Black women were redefining "the personal is political" in reaction to different kinds of stereotypes of "the strong (asexual) matriarchal Black woman." When the National Black Feminist Organization (NBFO) issued a statement of purpose in 1973, it asserted that Black women were a part of the women's liberation movement; that their seeming exclusion was only a construction of the white, male-dominated media.[22] As noted above, however, Black and white women were situated quite differently, historically and experientially, within left organizations in the 1960s and 1970s. Thus, ultimately, while the NBFO did identify as part of women's liberation, Black women in large part organized separately from white women's groups throughout the 1970s. Some understood their fight to be linked more with anti-imperialist women's struggles than with white women in the US. Others did not agree with the increasingly separatist strategies white women were adopting to organize as autonomously or "freely" from men.[23] For Black women, "the personal is political" eventually transformed into claims about identity and what came to be referred to as "identity politics." The struggle to claim a political identity in solidarity with Black men as oppressed by white supremacy and as women against masculinist myths of manhood framed the political lives of Black feminists.[24]

The differentiated terms on which Black feminists took up "the personal is political" were elaborated in the context of confronting the family as a political institution. The radical feminist critique, which politicized the family as an institution by arguing it could and should be radically transformed or even abolished if women's liberation was to be attained, did not resonate with Black feminists. Black women were less invested in this critique of the family and the terms of bourgeois masculinity that framed its presence and legitimacy. The legacy of slavery and Jim Crow left many families in Black communities fractured and fragile; the brutal separations of lovers, the prohibition on slave marriage, the selling away of children, and the intentional disempowerment and material impoverishment of Black people since Reconstruction made the very creation of a "family" an act of resistance. It also led to the emergence of alternative forms of "family."[25] Twentieth-century Black women were not escaping the constraints of white middle-class conformity and suburbia, as were white women; they criticized the state not for incentivizing and enforcing oppressive nuclear family values, but rather as complicit in destroying the potential for stable relationships among African American people and thus destroying Black children's futures. In this sense, the "personal" space of the family was critiqued as "political" for Black and white women, but for essentially different reasons that required very different strategies on the part of activists. The report titled "The Negro Family: The Case for National Action," overseen by Daniel Patrick Moynihan for the US Department of Labor in 1965, identified the predominance of female-headed households in Black families as creating a "matriarchal" society that diminished the likelihood of Black men committing to fatherhood.[26] The report displaced white responsibility for the condition of African American communities and neighborhoods onto the "culture" of Black women, families, and communities in the name of "rethinking" welfare policy. The report encouraged the proliferation of "culture of poverty" arguments that attribute the failure of Black communities to thrive to pathologies in family structure. This discursive construction of "cause and effect" illustrates the double burden Black women experience in politicizing the terms on which family is understood in the context of social-welfare liberalism.[27]

Feminism as requiring an intersectional approach to identity is discussed in Chapter 2. Here I discuss how that development is related to "the personal is political." The Combahee River Collective (CRC) Statement of 1983 translated "the personal is political" explicitly into a claim about the relationship between identity and experience: "Black women have always embodied, if only in their physical manifestation, an adversarial stance to white male rule and have actively resisted its inroads upon them and their communities in both dramatic and subtle ways." Further, the manifesto said:

> This focusing upon our own oppression is embodied in the concept of identity politics. We believe that the most profound and potentially most radical politics *come directly out of our own identity*, as opposed to working to end somebody else's oppression. In the case of Black women this is a particularly repugnant, dangerous, threatening, and therefore revolutionary concept because it is obvious from looking at all the political movements that have preceded us that anyone is more worthy of liberation than ourselves. We reject pedestals, queenhood, and walking ten paces behind. To be recognized as human, levelly human, is enough.[28]

This manifesto suggests that, in their very existence, Black women manifest resistance to white male rule. This echoes, albeit tangentially, Marx's claim that the working class, brought into existence by capitalism, will undo capitalism. As a socialist feminist organization, the CRC describes its analysis of the politics of Black women's situation as a critical reformulation. It does not present feminism, as some radical and cultural feminists did, as an autonomous theoretical or practical approach that would exhaustively capture sex oppression. This idea is elaborated when the statement directly addresses the idea that the personal is political. It gives an account of the multiple oppressions that Black women experience.

> A political contribution which we feel we have already made is the expansion of the feminist principle that the personal is political. In our consciousness-raising sessions, for example,

we have in many ways gone beyond white women's revelations because we are dealing with the implications of race and class as well as sex. Even our Black women's style of talking/testifying in Black language about what we have experienced has a resonance that is both cultural and political.[29]

It is by embodying an oppressed race, class, and gender, in the very form of their existence, that Black women are everything that threatens white, male, class-based rule. Here, the personal is political in a literal sense; it is in the personhood of the oppressed. It is a complex and embedded (in political history and differentiated contexts) sense of the "personal" that the manifesto describes.

In 1981, Bernice Johnson Reagon delivered what would become a widely read and anthologized speech about coalition in what had become the age of identity politics. She understood—as did early radical feminist groups—"the personal as political" as a means to organize for social change, not as a way to find safe spaces to abide in one's difference. Her metaphor for consciousness-raising groups, or what became by the early 1980s identity-based groups, was "home." But she destabilizes the idea of "home," reminding those at the Women's Music Festival—particularly white women—that if they attempt to keep their home homogenous, not only will they fail to make social change, but they will become an easy target, marked for destruction. Staying at "home" (in this case, as woman-identified women) would become a practice of exclusion and mimic the politics that inspired the movement in the first place.[30] Ultimately, Reagon's rhetoric invoked "the personal as political" as an inspirational source of activism rather than as a constative utterance. The personal is not the same as the political; it harbors the potentialities of the political—that is, a place of contestation over power and the terms of inclusion. Shane Phelan makes a similar argument as she critiques the tendency of feminists to aspire to authenticity in self and relations, thus losing site of the power relationships that cut across the category "woman."[31]

Like Reagon in "Turning the Century," in an address titled "The Master's Tools will Never Dismantle the Master's House" given in 1984, Audre Lorde says it is through acknowledging the dangerousness of racial differences that her predominantly white audience may find their creativity. But that danger lives in the self as much as it does in social relationships:

I agreed to take part in a New York University Institute for the Humanities conference a year ago, with the understanding that I would be commenting upon papers dealing with the role of difference within the lives of American women: difference of race, sexuality, class, and age. The absence of these considerations weakens any feminist discussion of the personal and the political.

She goes on to say:

Racism and homophobia are real conditions of all our lives in this place and time. I urge each one of us here to reach down into that deep place of knowledge inside herself and touch that terror and loathing of any difference that lives there. See whose face it wears. Then the personal as the political can begin to illuminate all our choices.[32]

Lorde calls for critical work on the self; she elaborates a transformative process of confrontation with biased aspects of the self too deeply rooted in and by historical circumstance and experience to be obvious. Thus, the personal as "identity" or "subjectivity" is a space of politics in itself requiring attention for those who aspire to lead a just and ethical life.

Thus far, we have seen that "the personal is political" is a claim about expanding the spaces that politics might be found, a proscriptive analytic, a prescriptive set of norms, a method for getting to a theory, and a means to self-transformation toward effective coalition-building and political struggle. It has been a starting point for internal critique and conflict among feminists and inspires the exploration of the self and subjectivity. Its mutability meant it would be taken up in different ways by different groups of feminists as it circulated in very different contexts and among different groups of women. The Redstockings Manifesto issues one classic interpretation:

Because we have lived so intimately with our oppressors, in isolation from each other, we have been kept from seeing our personal suffering as a political condition. This creates the impression that a woman's relationship with her man is a matter of interplay between two unique personalities and can be worked

out individually. In reality, every such relationship is a class relationship, and the conflict, between individual men and wom-
en are political conflicts that can only be solved collectively.[33]

As seen in the CRC Statement, "the personal is political" also informed what in the 1980s came to be called "identity politics," in
addition to inspiring theory and practices that challenge the private/
public divide.

"Identity politics" and "identity and difference" were common
references in feminist theorizing and practice by the late 1980s. In
"Identity: Skin, Blood, Heart," Minnie Bruce Pratt reflects on her
personal identity as a networked forcefield, littered with ethical and
political pitfalls.[34] She takes up Lorde's challenge in her everyday
life and chronicles the experience. Her essay ultimately argues that
an ethical individual will, with each encounter with "difference,"
acknowledge and reflect on a lesson that emerges from the personal
being political: that our identities are like a tapestry of tightly min-
gled threads, each of which may be alternatively threatening or subordinated in any given context. The autobiographical accounts in
the volume that include Pratt's essay, titled *Yours in Struggle*,[35] do
not seek authenticity in the self; nor do they attempt to gather up all
of the particularities and differences of the personal in order to
establish once and for all a unity as a necessary precondition for
politics. According to Chandra Mohanty and Biddy Martin, Pratt's
accomplishment is in her resistance to the conflation of her personal
experience, as such, with "the political" in such a way that the political significance of her identity is exhausted by unitary claims about
her victimization.[36] One could also describe Pratt's essay as elaborating a kind of lifelong consciousness-raising session as she navi-
gates through and resists a world constituted by differences, internal
and external to her self, created through histories of relationships of
dominance and power. Her essay reflects Reagon's wariness about
the desire to recreate "home" in our political lives when "homes"
are necessarily constituted through the exclusion of otherness and
difference and therefore resistant to the agonistic quality of
coalition-building and political change.

Kimberlé Crenshaw argues that feminist research should start
from the assumption that identities forged in oppressive relationships do not exist parallel to one another. Instead, they "intersect"

in the subjective and objective lives of women as subjects, and it is
this point of intersection that feminism should struggle to articulate.
Her work builds on many insights feminist activists and thinkers
developed in the 1980s about identity, while highlighting blind
spots about the "personal" in some feminist organizing against
domestic violence and anti-discrimination law. Crenshaw challenges liberalism's imperative to empty social and cultural, or
"identity differences," of meaning in order to achieve a society of
tolerance and, ultimately, sameness. But she goes on to say:

> Yet implicit in certain strands of feminist and racial liberation
> movements, for example, is the view that the social power in
> delineating difference need not be the power of domination; it
> can instead be the source of social empowerment and recon-
> struction.[37]

The politics of difference here does not have to be left to the sorting
powers of the dominant class. It is subject to the concrete reclamation
Lorde calls for when she says political power lies in acknowledging
buried fears of being different or encountering difference. Crenshaw
describes the differences between women of color and white wom-
en in the context of domestic violence. As in the discussion above
of the differences in the personal experiences of Black women and
white women in the family, Crenshaw identifies the ways anti-
violence discourses and strategies on the part of feminist and anti-racist groups form in such a way as to render the experiences of
women of color unintelligible. She uses the language of "location,"
"experience," and "identity," rather than "personal," to invoke the
specificity of the subject of her analysis (women of color).

Crenshaw's examples illustrate the racist and classist maldistri-
butions of state resources resulting from the elision of women of
color from predominant constructions of the problem. It is not
merely a "personal" or privatized problem—though it is certainly
that—but is intertwined with issues of citizenship, racist policing
strategies, the sexualization of Black female bodies, the criminalization of Black male bodies, and access to resources more generally. To construct the issue of rape and domestic violence as about
rescuing women from the traditional constraints of liberal privacy
in the middle-class nuclear family elides the intersecting ways

citizenship status, race, religious values, and resources alter the meanings of and the reactions to the harms done to women in various sites in which they live, work, play or wander.

"THE PERSONAL IS POLITICAL" AND THE PRIVATE/ PUBLIC DISTINCTION

The phrase "the personal is political" as an axiomatic reference has influenced feminist theorizing from standpoint theory, which asks how lived experience inflects knowledge production and perceptions of reality[38]; to body politics, which interrogates how embodied characteristics or behaviors are symptomatic of gendered, sexed, and racialized constructions of difference[39]; to critical social psychology, which assumes interpersonal relations are effects of power relationships, not a neutral process of socialization or role development.[40] Preconceptions governing the sense of personhood, or pertaining to our self, are politicized in the sense that they are shown to be effects of, not causes of, constructions of gendered, sexed, and racial differences. Liberal constructions of what is appropriately available for political contestation have been challenged by feminisms inspired by the possibilities of contesting oppressively personalized and individuated conditions of life. Feminist critiques of the public/private divide have argued for reconfigurations of the relationship between the personal and political that do not reify either term as unchangeable or sacred.

As is shown in discussions of contemporary feminist books about feminisms in the next chapter, the personal as a particular space of individualized and/or familial "privacy" is unique to Western modernity. On the one hand, feminist literature that builds on the personal being politicized shows that there is nothing primeval, organic, or immutable about the personal or private spaces in which we "find ourselves" or build personalities. The "personal" is never and never has been immune to public/political intervention, scrutiny, judgment, sanction, or misrecognition.

Linda Nicholson identifies the phrase as a significant rebuttal of liberal and Marxist theories, both of which assume the family to be an ahistorical fact, ontologically prior to and distinct from the sphere of politics and economic relations of production.[41] John Locke, discussed in Chapter 2, situates the equalitarian space of his polity against the "naturally" patriarchal space of the family. Marxism projects the possibility that the "personal," defined as the capacity to consciously produce the whole of nature in freedom, will ultimately be unbound from the bourgeois mythology about the home as the space of freedom and autonomy. Liberalism distinguishes the bases for relationships in the family—those being nature, honor, and duty—from those of the polity, reason, contract, and self-interest. Marx and Marxism understand that production moved, with the advent of capitalism, from the household to the factory and that, in fact, there was nothing sacred or natural about the condition of the family in capitalism. However, in the Marxist analyses of that movement, the family becomes an anachronism whose justifications are historically rendered irrelevant by the imperatives of capital.

Nicholson's purpose is to argue that the "personal" as that which is private or non-political must be understood to be in a historical dynamic with what is considered political at any given time. Nicholson argues for the historicity of that which is personal or privatized, critiquing those feminist approaches that seek out causative origins of "patriarchy," or gendered and/or sexed conditions of inequality and domination. The personal as "privacy" is unique to Western modernity. As a response to patriarchal norms that reify the public/private distinction as natural and necessary to the future of a stable democratic republic, "the personal is political" was taken up as a critique of the public/private divide. Feminists argue that nothing considered "personal" should be immune to judgment about its collusion with oppression or harm or injustice.

CONCLUSION

The Vagina Monologues is a recent incarnation of "the personal is political." The movement begun by V's (written when "V" identified as Eve Ensler) play insists on talking about the vagina in public and without shame: about what happens to "it"; what "it" likes and does not like; and why, as a body part, "it" has been subject to such bizarre claims and damaging treatment over the ages and across time. The international success of *The Vagina Monologues* may be due, in part, to the fact that it renders public that body part that has been alternatively violently objectified or mystified by patriarchy while also being a source of pleasure.[42]

The originality of the play lies in putting an otherwise "hidden" or "secret" body part, rather than a marginalized identity, at the center of political attention. It acknowledges the vagina as mutable in its significance and as having political standing as a measure of the freedom (and even pleasures) that should be available in the world. Radical feminist groups reintroduced women to their vaginas in the 1970s. But they did not introduce the vagina with the public as an audience. Critiques of *The Vagina Monologues* (not so much the international movement that has taken it up as a rallying cry) focus our attention back onto the potential for essentialism and artificial unity in "woman"—or in this case, in identifying through a body part held in common, implicit in the phrase "the personal is political." Christine Cooper points out that most configurations of the monologues performed use "the raped Bosnian woman" to stand in for "traditional societies" and third (or second)-world brutality.[43] *The Vagina Monologues* is not some kind of endgame in the history of "the personal is political"; while identifying through the vagina carries the historical baggage of the patriarchal identification of "woman" with the body and sexuality, it also acts as a rhetorical reclamation of a body part that has, in part because of the "personal" and "private" (secret and hidden) quality of its existence, been available to be vilified culturally and brutalized physically. A genealogy of the journey of *The Vagina Monologues* over the two decades that saw it produced in hundreds of significantly revised versions reflects how feminisms are persistently self-critical and consistently unpacking biases, essentialisms; the history of *The Vagina Monologues* is emblematic of how feminisms shift and change over time in response to internal critique and popular responses.

There are many other examples how "the personal is political" plays in the contemporary context. It does not resonate in the same way as when it was invoked in the name of political resistance to privatized dominance and oppression. Challenges to uproot, disrupt, disclaim, or disaggregate normative identity formations, assumptions, and relationships have become claims to rights for marginalized persons and groups (e.g., "gay liberation" now means the right to same-sex marriage). In another iteration, the original meanings of the phrase have disappeared into "choice feminism." In "choice feminism," the personal is political because an individual woman now has a choice about enacting femininity; her style and decisions are "choices" and therefore, in themselves, are empty of political content aside from the triumphalist contrast with a less enlightened past.

At the most basic level, second-wave feminism was (is?) about showing that those choices that liberalism and now neoliberalism think of as "personal" are actually socially constructed and act as constraints on our capacities. Much of the ire raised among public commentators about feminism (from Rush Limbaugh to those who advocate "choice") is that it dares to judge what "ought to be" left to personal preferences. It judges as Linda Hirshman did in 2006 when she made an argument that women with high-powered educations should stay in the workforce and shape the world differently than it is.[44] It judges as womyn-identified women did when they challenged self-identified feminists who were intimate with men to reflect on whether they were attuned to the dynamics of compulsive heterosexuality as an institution. It judges as radical feminists did when they protested the Miss America Pageant in Atlantic City in 1968. Feminisms are political movements in that they make judgments about a world in which staying home to care for children, sleeping with men, or competing for public recognition and resources on the basis of skin tone and shiny teeth (made so by smearing Vaseline on the teeth, which also made the smile slide more easily across the face) are not "real" choices (whatever that may mean). It demands we question whether we are making choices, falling off the log of habit or second nature, or defending ourselves from sanction and abuse. Feminisms are about judging "personal behavior" in that they assess the context in which that personal behavior is naturalized and normative. The question is not whether feminisms make "correct" judgments. It is about feminisms exposing otherwise unseen and/or untouchable sites for judgment. Feminisms make us pay attention to the discursive and material context of "choices" rather than assuming the choice is self-evident based on individual desire or purpose.[45]

Through the influence of new social movements and radical rethinking of the "personal," the significance of equality and justice was brought into the space of the personal. Inequality does not just have socioeconomic impacts on communities affected by discrimination, oppression, exclusion, marginalization, and violence. It renders the personal, as related to the person and personhood, necessarily political. The influence of liberal individualism has trivialized the meaning of this recognition. The accusations of "cancel culture" or "wokeness" suggest claims of harm are, instead, neurotic symptoms. There is a difference between taking discrimination as a personal "offense" that should be compensated and politicizing that personalized or individualized experience by showing how it is informed by normative assumptions and unthought relationships of dominance. Politicizing acts of discrimination should highlight not the impact on the individual and demands for compensation, but the implications for the way we as a now global community have lived (survived) and will live together. As heterosexual relationships are no longer the invisible norm, but instead something that require explanation (the peculiar questions asked about homosexuality could be turned on heterosexuality to good rhetorical effect: is there a heterosexual gene? What makes heterosexual intimacy more "real"?), the world changes—and not only because individuals will live with less fear. Rather, it changes because the formation of the "personal" is never untouched by the meaning and significance of what is recognizable, legitimately present and valued, or rendered possible in the public/political spaces we inhabit together.

The next chapter reviews contemporary feminist discussions of feminisms. Each in its own way reminds us that the personal is political. Once argued as such, there is often violent reaction in a global context in which male dominance is still very much in place. Moruzzi's study of reformist women in Iran in the 1990s illustrates the point. However, the personal cannot be unseen as political once it is exposed as a space where dominance oppresses and power relations shape possibilities for particular people identified as feminine, female, or as otherwise excluded from the traditional political space. Rendering the personal political remains a critical part of how feminisms theorize, demand, and enact progressive social change.

NOTES

1 Moruzzi, Claire, *Tied Up in Tehran: Women, Social Change, and Everyday Life in Post-Revolutionary Iran* (Cambridge University Press, 2025) 32.

2 "New social movements" refers to the emergence of multiple organized liberation movements in the 1960s and 1970s. The appellation refers to organizations that do not take class conflict as the singular or fundamental point

of departure for analysis of social and political oppressions. An emphasis on "identity" and the constitutive qualities of race, gender, sexuality, ability, and ethnicity expanded the possibilities for understanding dominance and subordination in the social order.

3 Evans, Sara, *Personal Politics: The Roots of the Women's Liberation in the Civil Rights Movement and the New Left* (Vintage Books, 1980).

4 The SSOC was founded when white activists were no longer welcome in the SNCC.

5 Evans, ibid 40.

6 Evans, ibid 57.

7 Breines, Winifred, *The Trouble Between Us: An Uneasy History of White and Black Women in the Feminist Movement* (Oxford University Press, 2006).

8 Hayden, Casey and Mary King, "A Kind of Memo," Chicago Women's Liberation Union Herstory Project. https://www.cwluherstory.org/classic-feminist-writings-articles/a-kind-of-memo. The original document was distributed in 1965. It was uploaded here in 2022.

9 Ibid.

10 In *Daring to be Bad* (University of Minnesota Press, 1984), Alice Echols points out that at a 1967 meeting, the National Conference for a New Politics, Todd Gitlin referred to the acceptance of the meeting of Black demands for control of SNCC as the "castration" of the white male. "Castrated whites will not create a movement worthy of alliance" (p. 313). Echols mentions this with little comment. However, the unconscious identification of the movement as essentially male and the implication that Black men were castrating white men are both profoundly insulting to white and Black women and to the history of torture and castration Black men experienced at the hands of white slaveholders and mobs. It is telling that the joking comment made by Stokely Carmichael in the tense aftermath of an early presentation of women's claims at a SNCC meeting that "the position of women in SNCC is prone" has traveled so much further in historical memory. Echols puts this comment in context, showing us that Carmichael was parodying his own sexism, not making a misogynist claim about women in the movement (p. 31). The distorted meaning of Stokely Carmichael's comment travels as evidence of the sexism in the leadership of SNCC, while Todd Gitlin's very straightforwardly racist and sexist comment escapes notice.

11 Koedt, Ann, Ellen Levine and Anita Rapone, *Radical Feminism* (Times Books, 1973) 282–284; 285–289.

12 Snitow, Ann, "A Gender Diary," in *The Feminism of Uncertainty: A Gender Diary* (Duke University Press, 2015), https://read.dukeupress.edu/books/book/181/chapter-abstract/107204/A-Gender-Diary?redirectedFrom=PDF https://doi.org/10.1215/9780822375678.

13 Gavey, Nicole, *Just Sex: The Cultural Scaffolding of Rape* (Routledge, 2005/2018).

14 The New York City-based radical feminist group Redstockings organized a protest and speak-out during the legislative hearing about the legalization of abortion in New York state.

15 The first "Take Back the Night" rally was in Philadelphia, Pennsylvania in 1977. The mission of the now international event has transformed to contest the terms of violence more generally, but sustains its original focus of sexual violence and women's freedom of movement.

16 Hasday, Jill Elaine, "Contest and Consent: A Legal History of Marital Rape" in *California Law Review* vol. 88 5 (2000).

17 MacKinnon, Catharine, *Sexual Harassment of Working Women: A Case of Discrimination* (Yale University Press, 1986).

18 Estrich, Susan, *Real Rape: How the Legal System Victimizes Women Who Say No* (Harvard University Press, 1988).

19 Ferguson, Ann, et al. "Sex War: The Debate between Radical and Libertarian Feminists" in *Signs* vol. 10 1 (1984) 106–112.

20 Snitow, Ann, Christine Stansell, and Sharon Thompson, *Powers of Desire: The Politics of Sexuality* (Monthly Review Press, 1983); and Vance, Carol, *Pleasure and Danger* (Pandora Press, 1984).

21 Rubin, Gayle, "Thinking Sex: Notes for a Radical Theory of Sexuality" in Carole S. Vance (ed.) *Pleasure and Danger* (Pandora Press, 1984).

22 NBFO, "Statement of Purpose" in Penny A. Weiss (ed.) *Feminist Manifestos: A Global Documentary Reader* (New York University Press, 2018).

23 Allen, Pam, *Free Space: A Perspective on the Small Group in Women's Liberation* (Times Change Press, 2000).

24 Wallace, Michelle, *Black Macho and the Myth of the Superwoman* (Caldor Publications, 1979); Hull, Gloria, Patricia Scott and Gloria Smith, *All the Women are White, All the Blacks are Men, But Some of us are Brave* (The Feminist Press, 1982).

25 Collins, Patricia Hill, *Black Feminist Thought* (Taylor and Francis, 1990).

26 Moynihan, Daniel Patrick, *The Negro Family: The Case for National Action*, Office of Policy Planning and Research, U.S. Department of Labor (U.S. Government Printing Office, March 1965).

27 Giddings, Paula, *When and Where I Enter: The Impact of Black Women on Race and Sex in America* (William and Morrow, 1984).

28 The Combahee River Collective Statement is reprinted at https://www.blackpast.org/african-american-history/combahee-river-collective-statement-1977/.

29 Ibid.

30 Reagon, Bernice Johnson, "Coalition Politics: Turning the Century" in Barbara Smith (ed.) *Home Girls: A Black Feminist Anthology* (Kitchen Table-Woman of Color Press, 1983).

31 Phelan, Shane, "The Jargon of Authenticity: Adorno and Feminist Essentialism" in *Philosophy and Social Criticism* vol. 16 1 (1990) 39–54.

32 Lorde, Audre "The Master's Tools Will Never Dismantle the Master's House" in *Sister/Outsider Essays and Speeches* (Crossing Press, 1984) 11.

33 Crow, Barbara (ed.) *Radical Feminism: A Documentary Reader* (New York University Press, 2000).

34 Pratt, Minnie Bruce, "Identity, Skin, Blood, Heart" in Elly Bulkin, Barbara Smith, and Minnie Bruce Pratt (eds.) *Yours in Struggle* (Long Haul Press, 1984).

35 Bulkin, Elly, Barbara Smith, and Minnie Bruce Pratt (eds.) *Yours in Struggle: Three Feminist Perspectives on Anti-Semitism and Racism* (Firebrand Books, 1984).

36 Mohanty, Chandra and Biddy Martin, "What's Home Got to Do with It?" in *Feminism Without Borders: Decolonizing Theory, Practicing Solidarity* (Duke University Press, 2003).

37 Crenshaw, Kimberlé, "Mapping the Margins: Intersectionality, Feminism, and Violence Against Women" in *Stanford Law Review* vol. 43 6 (1991).

38 Hartsock, Nancy, *Money, Sex and Power: Toward a Feminist Historical Materialism* (Northeastern University Press, 1985).

39 Young, Iris, "The Ideal of Community and the Politics of Difference" in *Social Theory and Practice* vol. 12 1 (1986).

40 Henley, Nancy, "The Sexual Politics of Interpersonal Behavior" in Jo Freeman (ed.) *Women: A Feminist Perspective*, 5th edition (McGraw Hill, 1994).

41 Nicholson, Linda, *Gender and History: The Limits of Social Criticism in the Age of the Family* (Columbia University Press, 1985).

42 Ensler, Eve, *The Vagina Monologues* (Dramatists Play Service, 2000).

43 Cooper, Christine, "Worrying about Vaginas: Feminism and Eve Ensler's Vagina Monologues" in *Signs* vol. 32 3 (2007) 727–758.

44 Hirshman, Linda, *Get to Work: A Manifesto for Women of the World* (Viking, 2006).

45 Marzo, Lori, "Feminism's Quest for Common Desires" in *Perspectives in Politics* vol. 8 1 (2010).

5

CONTEMPORARY FEMINISTS ON FEMINISMS

INTRODUCTION

In this chapter, I explore what several contemporary self-identified feminists say about feminism. I have selected these particular texts because the authors make self-conscious efforts to write in an accessible or popular, as distinct from "academic," way about feminism. This does not mean these texts have reached a massive audience, or that they are "popular" in the sense of being appreciated. They are public in the sense that the authors self-consciously attempt to write for and address the public at large. I will call them "public-facing" feminist texts.

The authors are journalists, academics, activists, and independent writers, each wearing several of these hats. I identify how/ whether they (1) relate to feminisms as described in Chapter 2; (2) pose a few critical questions about their approach to and claims about feminism; and (3) show how they sharpen the critical edges and reflective quality of the field of thought and action that characterizes feminism. No one has the right answer to the questions "What is feminism?" or "What is a feminist?" Rather, we should read these texts for what they help us understand about the possibilities, dilemmas, and problems of feminism and being a feminist in the contemporary moment.

Many public-facing books about feminism are reflections on the authors' own lives and journeys. They cross over between interpretation/analysis and autobiography. The personal is political in these texts. The authors show how what we typically think of as individual voices and choices reflect political principles, both in

DOI: 10.4324/9781003264682-5

the sense of being shaped by the "common sense" of any given historical context and in the sense of desiring to shape/change that common sense. They should be understood as seeking out the *public good.*

FEMINISM AND NEOLIBERALISM

In her 2018 book, *Empowered: Popular Feminism and Popular Misogyny*, Sarah Banet-Weiser identifies what she calls "popular feminism."[1] I noted in Chapter 1 that feminism has surfaced over the last 20 years and across the globe as a "popular" phenomenon. We see the term across the internet being attached to sales of t-shirts, mugs, and stickers; and being used by pop-culture personalities and female corporate leaders leading confidence-building workshops. If the term itself is not explicitly on display, assertions of female-specific empowerment in a "man's world" imply it. However, Banet-Weiser distinguishes between this popular feminism and a feminism that demands change in the structures, institutions, policies, oppressive norms, and gendered habits that sustain the conditions in which females require empowerment in the first place. She identifies popular feminism with *neoliberalism.*

I have discussed liberalism at length and referenced it quite often as a default position of many feminists working in institutional spaces in the 20th century. I will point to liberal tendencies in the discussions of books that follows here. *Neo*liberalism, however, is quite different from this liberalism with its focus on individuality, rights, and equality as principles through which we organize ourselves politically.

Neoliberalism places its faith in market forces and individual initiative. It associates *freedom* with individualized economic activity; political interventions in economic activity are not merely bad policy in instrumental terms—they deprive individuals of fundamental freedoms to act according to their individual capacities and desires. Self-identified neoliberals call for divestment from public institutions and the privatization of what classical liberals would identify as public obligations (e.g., schools, prisons, or regulatory agencies). More importantly for our purposes here, neoliberalism identifies our individuality and personhood with economic initiative. It is not only about investing money, time, energy or talents in a business or other activity; individuals literally invest *in themselves* in order to maximize the worth of their appearance, talents, life experience, or assets. Individuals become brands. For example, applicants for jobs are encouraged not only to list their abilities and talents, but to sell themselves as a brand to employers.[2]

Neoliberalism suggests all of one's possessions—one's self, home, and car—become potential investments. We rent spaces in our homes and use our cars as taxis. These traditionally private spaces and our personalities as Airbnb hosts or Uber drivers become marketable brands, commodities to be bought and sold. Further, as individuals, we become inseparable from our brand and what we sell as such. As Jay Z famously said: "I am not a businessman. I'm a business, man."[3] The same could be said by and of Beyoncé, Taylor Swift, and other individuals who have such an outsized cultural presence that managing their image, celebrity, and cultural production is an industry unto itself.

Ultimately, Banet-Weiser identifies popular feminism as feeding a market-obsessed neoliberal culture, not something that challenges the market as a space of material exploitation or cultural/social oppression. It is hard to argue against empowering girls and women to become economically successful in the "man's world" of the marketplace. However, this reduction of the meaning and purpose of feminism to individual success, including individual women's capacity to control their own image in the marketplace, cannot capture either the complexity of intersectional meaning that representations of masculinity and femininity carry with them or the actual fact, historically, that while individual cultural icons and leaders capture our attention, it is through collective political action that progressive changes happen for all women.

The feminists and feminisms I discuss in this chapter are not the "popular feminisms" described and criticized by Banet-Weiser, but they do aspire to reach a wide audience. They do not prioritize the success of individual women and girls in a marketplace that perpetuates oppression and exploitation. Rather, they deconstruct the foundational terms on which gender, race, sexuality, class and other vectors of oppression and exploitation make it harder for girls and women as such to flourish. They give names to their feminist sensibilities to capture the cultural and political moments they are living in and through. Their commentary is deeply informed by the feminisms described in this book and beyond. They sometimes use "we" as a collective reference, "I" as an autobiographical reference, and "you" as a form of authorial address to an assumed audience. And they navigate and reflect the conflicting moral, political, and cultural claims of many feminisms that have gone before in terms of how we should think about what it is to be a feminist. As is the case with all feminisms, much of the contemporary discussion revolves around issues of sexuality, representations of the sexual/sexualized gendered body, and questions about family and kinship obligations. They respond to and critique arguments and demands of feminists that have gone before, moving from their lived contemporary experiences and contexts as activists, writers, journalists, and academic into arguments about representation and activism.

BRITTNEY COOPER AND THE CRUNK FEMINIST COLLECTIVE

> Have you ever noticed that those with power and wealth and influence do not attend and have not attended empowerment seminars?
> Brittney Cooper[4]

Brittney Cooper is a Black Feminist (she capitalizes both terms to emphasize the both-and quality of her commitments) scholar who writes for academic audiences and for broader audiences. Like many feminists, she wants her thinking to be accessible to a wide range of readers. *Eloquent Rage: A Black Feminist Discovers her Superpower*, published in 2018,[5] narrates how she came to feminism as a Black woman and how she wants to (re)shape feminism to include what she calls the messiness of a person like her.

Her rage at the conditions in which Black women and girls survive and thrive and fail in the gendered-raced context of the US is Cooper's point of departure. She wants to politicize what otherwise she experiences as an ephemeral and generalized feeling. In her introduction, she says she wants to render her rage precise and targeted, the way Serena and Venus Williams render their power and strength in a 120-mile-per-hour shot across a tennis court net.

The book is autobiographical, but every story from Cooper's life works to develop the reader's understanding of what Cooper identifies as Black Feminism. The narrative is simultaneously therapeutic, cultural, and political. She moves from the very personal—childhood friendships, moments with her mother, crushes on other kids—to an argument about, in this case, the importance of Black female friendship, love, and loyalty, at all ages, to sustaining a Black Feminist politics.

Much of the book is focused on untangling racialized and sexed encounters among family and community members, friends, and colleagues. Using as evidence stories and descriptions of experiences of Black women, including her own, Cooper lays out what progressive changes in attitudes and behaviors would look like. Black men would respect Black women as individuals beyond the expectations of roles such as mother, wife, or sister. Everyone would respect Black women without expecting them to be "respectable," as in, modeling white patterns of behavior and measures of success. White women would rise up at harms against Black women. White women would hold one another accountable for the fact that 53% of white women voted for Donald Trump, who embodies and explicitly celebrates white supremacist misogyny. Black women would love one another unconditionally because Black women deserve love in a context where they are assumed to be the problem as a group ("single moms" and "welfare queens") while simultaneously expected to be unreasonably heroic as individuals.

Following on Banet-Weiser's critique of neoliberal expectations of the individual, Cooper distinguishes between the language of "empowerment" and that of "power." She says:

> Empowerment looks like cultivating the wisdom to make the best choices we can out of what are customarily a piss-poor set of options. Power looks like the ability to create better options. The powerlessness and capriciousness of being repeatedly jammed up at the personal and political crossroads of one's intersections while a watching world pretends not to see you there, needing help, is how it feels to be a Black woman on an ordinary day.[6]

Cooper's book, *Eloquent Rage*, was published shortly after her more academically inclined study of Black women and respectability politics. In *Beyond Respectability: the Intellectual Thought of*

Race Women,[7] Cooper shows how Black women activist/thinkers in the post-Reconstruction US self-consciously deployed and criticized respectability politics as they spoke out about the conditions and possibilities of Black Americans coming out of conditions of slavery. Respectability politics names the contradictory imperative of white supremacy that African Americans live up to the expectations of the white gaze even while the white supremacist order fails at every turn to acknowledge that Black lives matter. In this study, Cooper traces how Black women self-consciously enact respectability politics while facing down white supremacist misogyny.

> Respectability politics are at their core a rage-management project. Learning to manage one's rage by daily tamping down that rage is a response to routine assaults on one's dignity in a world where rage might get you killed or cause you to lose your job.[8]

Cooper does not read respectability politics as a "sellout" to the disciplinary imperatives of whiteness. And it is more than a survival tactic. It is a rage-management project. Black women tamp down their rage and channel it through public style and expression. In *Eloquent Rage,* Cooper describes Michelle Obama's hairstyle at Trump's inauguration—a ponytail/bun—as exemplary of this self-conscious rage-management project. Cooper explains the depth and value of Black women's hair vocabulary. That Obama did not "do" her hair—that she pushed it back, simply "ready to go and be elsewhere," given who was walking into the White House, not worrying about what those present thought—was an act of eloquent rage. Michelle Obama's presentation and enactment of herself as a Black woman speak to her rage about the conditions that allowed a figure like Trump to be elected; they are deeply political. They do not merely appear as a preference for a certain style. It may be a rhetorical flourish when Cooper says this was the day that respectability politics went out the window, but it represents a critical understanding of the significance of appearance and affect in politics.[9]

Cooper's appreciation for and critique of respectability politics, her "eloquent rage," and her attachment to Southern-style hip-hop inspired her and several friends, while in graduate school, to begin blogging as the Crunk Feminist Collective. They revived the effort in 2010 and published a volume collecting their essays in 2016.[10]

Southern-style hip-hop was/is the soundtrack for their Black Feminism. Hip hop provides visceral joy in sound and movement, metaphors, and community for Black feminists of the Crunk Collective. Crunk feminism is described by Brittney Cooper in the preface to the *Crunk Feminist Collection*: "Our work is fueled by the notion of the percussive—when you put crunk beside feminism you don't get a sweet melody but rather a productive and compelling dissonance."[11] Inspired in part by Joan Morgan's book *When Chickenheads Come Home to Roost: A Hip Hop Feminist Breaks it Down*,[12] the Crunk Collective says their feminism contends with the gray area between what they agree with in claims by some Black feminists about the misogyny endemic to hip-hop and the desire to "live large," aware of and outspoken about the misogyny but also of the joy in the beat and the feel, erotic and otherwise, of the artform. Crunk feminism celebrates female desire, which is not pure or predictable, and reflects and challenges the culture that shapes it. In *Eloquent Rage,* Cooper says:

> Now I am a grown woman trying to build a life where I can get in bed every night with a man who knows that my desire for him to hold me down does not in any guise mean that I want him to put his foot on my neck.[13]

Creating and performing hip-hop, Black male artists accuse Black women of attitudes imbued with white supremacist ideology,[14] while Black feminist commentary calls out Black male artists for the same.[15] bell hooks described gangsta rap, and later hip-hop, as Black youth laboring on the plantation of patriarchal, white supremacist, capitalist culture. Joan Morgan, on the other hand, wants a feminism ". . . that would allow me to explore who we are as women—not victims. One that claimed the powerful richness and delicious complexities inherent in being black girls now—sistas of the post-Civil Rights, post-feminist, post soul, hip-hop generation."[16] Morgan and the hip-hop feminists inspired by her work focus on Black female desire and agency to recreate themselves in the face of what bell hooks calls white supremacist patriarchal capitalism. And part of the desire hip-hop feminism "fucks with" is those male habits traditional feminisms consider symptoms of male dominance. Morgan wants a feminism that can "admit that part of the reason women love hip-hop—as sexist as it is—is 'cuz all that in-yo-face testosterone makes our nipples hard?"[17]

Morgan's book advises about setting boundaries, loving rappers from a distance, loving the music but not all the messages, and asking questions of the artists and fans as to why Black women are the objects of hatred and scorn. She refuses to take misogyny as a necessary part of the package but loves the package nonetheless because hip-hop is a space for exposure and healing of pain in the Black community. Interestingly, this book hardly discusses hip-hop as such. It is not a book of music criticism. She does not interpret lyrics or personality types of artists or the historical context of the emergence of hip-hop. Morgan writes her lived experience while drawing on a wealth of 1990s literature about relationships to articulate a feminism that itself is *doing* what hip-hop does: it expresses pain, joy, suffering, pleasure, anger, love, desire, acting as a mirror to the conditions in which Black people live in the US. It is contradictory and messy, not linear (progressive or regressive) or systematic in its analysis.

The book advises on cultural and individual strategies in the context of what Patricia Hill Collins calls the matrix of domination.[18] Morgan's book is an effort to write in a context in which, as discussed throughout this book, there exists a credibility gap into which Black women's voices are persistently pushed. What Brittney Cooper, following in a tradition of Black feminist criticism, discusses as respectability politics is the effort to attain credibility in the matrix of white, misogynist, classist contexts. That credibility gap does not provide the narrow ledges of presumed innocence and purity some white women can take advantage of as they speak out about their experiences of harm or pain or suffering. Black women speak, continually and everywhere; the issue is whether and how Black women are heard. Hence the emphasis in Cooper's and Morgan's public-facing feminist book on expression, style, presence, and syntax.

The Crunk Collective follows Joan Morgan's 1999 callout for a hip-hop feminism that "fucks with the grey area"[19] of Black female desires and Black masculinities. "Crunk" refers to the sound and feel of music—the heavy bass and hard-driving beats that characterize Southern hip-hop. It recognizes that women's desires are complex and that expectations of purity/respectability are tools of white bourgeois male dominance. Crunk feminism articulates alternatives to the bad habits lived out and normalized in the matrix of dominance while not repressing the desire to be bad. It consciously situates itself within the contradictory lived consequences of intersectional oppression.

The feminism that is crunk is anti-patriarchal. In the 1990s, there was a great deal of skepticism among feminists about naming "the patriarchy" as a feminist target. Use of the term "patriarchy" suggested a monolithic, totalized, structural space to be revolutionized, not a space with gaps and fissures in its logic, which often works against its own interests. "Patriarchy" as a feminist term was critiqued as an unnuanced reference point from which to develop a politics, but Crunk feminists do not hesitate to use and redefine the term. "Patriarchy is invested in the normalization of masculinity in all of its manifestations (including rape culture and violence) and the silence and invisibility of women, especially women of color."[20] This quote situates patriarchy as an aspiration ("invested in") and masculinity "in all of its manifestations" as a tool, yet Black masculinity is addressed in a nuanced and affective manner by Crunk feminism. It is a problem for Black feminism because they are writing about how to build relationships, intimate and otherwise, grounded in respect, which Black men and women must cultivate with one another. The thing is, as Joan Morgan says in no uncertain terms in *Chickenheads*, as misogynist as some expressions of Black masculinity may be, it is also sexy. Is this false consciousness on the part of those who are turned on? Is there an alternative authentic desire that would be anti-patriarchal if only we (women) could access/find/discover it? These are questions feminists have been asking for decades. Crunk feminism brings the questions back in the name of, once again, not allowing what bell hooks identifies as the patriarchal white supremacist capitalist system define the meaning of cultural representations for Black women. Black women will take up these cultural representations and say what they feel and know about them in all of their contradictory, messy, sentient, and ratchet (beyond respectability) fashions.

Respect, not "respectability," is a theme throughout the essays in the collection. Crunk feminism and ratchet feminisms perform dis-respectability in re-reading representations of Black female thought, subjectivity, bodies, sexuality, and desire that otherwise expose Blackness to moral judgements about excess. Black women are considered by white supremacist culture to be too angry, too sexual, too controlling—just "too much" in general. Crunk feminism is about finding space to be in this contradictory morass of representation.

Anger and rage are typically understood as emotional responses. In traditional political theory, emotions are distinct from politics and, according to some, undermine the capacity of collectives to engage rationally with one another to come to conclusions. The emphasis on "civic (civil) discourse often works to the detriment of those whose very existence has not been acknowledged as "civic" but as private and/or bound up with the irrationality of familial love or biological necessity. Feminists have challenged the dichotomy between emotion and rationality assumed in traditional political theory. They point out that political change happens when anger about oppressive conditions drives people to "act out"—whether those people be the revolutionaries of 1776 in the US or 1789 in France. Anger is intertwined with the political. Rebecca Traister's book *Good and Mad: the Revolutionary Power of Women's Anger*[21] traces the history of women's angry—even furious—responses to male obliviousness, disdain, and scorn when women challenge gender injustices.

There is a difference between anger driven by irrational fear of losing what one thinks one has, which drives white supremacist rage against emergent Black citizens or masculinist rage against women's increasing public presence, and anger driven by experiences and analysis of injustice and structurally unequal distributions of resources. The eloquent rage Cooper describes is channeled. It is not reactive, but constructive and pointed. Like Michelle Obama's hair at the inauguration of Donald Trump, it affectively and effectively targets injustice, speaking out in many complex forms and unexpected places.

SARA AHMED, *LIVING A FEMINIST LIFE*[22]

Ahmed's book reads like a transcript of a consciousness-raising session taking place in one person's head. She writes as she thinks, back and forth, with the voices from whom she has learned and with whom she has acted as a feminist. We all have multiple voices in our heads: ideas, messages, events, relationships with people and other living beings speak to us. Feminisms' many voices emerge in Ahmed's writing in this book. Like Cooper, she is an academic; she has published extensively in fields of feminist philosophy but with this book, she writes for a wider audience. Like Cooper, she is writing from her life experience. However, she does this differently as she enmeshes her life experience in her theorizing and advice about what it is to live a feminist life so completely that her personal narratives fade in and out as the text moves along. She is deeply involved in "thinking as she is doing," not contemplating action as something about which she wishes to comment or theorize. This makes the book read like stream of consciousness, with assertions interrupting the flow rather than summaries or transitions from one theme to another.

When it comes to defining "feminism," Ahmed emphasizes the need to remain uncertain, to avoid righteousness about what is or is not feminist, to sustain openness.[23] On the other hand, she later identifies bell hooks' definition as her point of departure:

> I want to take here bell hooks's definition of feminism as "the movement to end sexism, sexual exploitation and sexual oppression" (2000, 33). From this definition, we learn so much. Feminism is necessary because of what has not ended: sexism, sexual exploitation, and sexual oppression. And for hooks, "sexism, sexual exploitation and sexual oppression" cannot be separated from racism, from how the present is shaped by colonial histories including slavery, as central to the exploitation of labor under capitalism. Intersectionality is a starting point, the point from which we must proceed if we are to offer an account of how power works. Feminism will be intersectional "or it will be bullshit," to borrow from the eloquence of Flavia Dzodan.[24]

With respect to activity, Ahmed says:

> To be a feminist at work is or should be about how we challenge ordinary and everyday sexism, including academic sexism. This is not optional: it is what makes feminism feminist. A feminist project is to find ways in which women can exist in relation to women; how women can be in relation to each other. It is a project because we are not there yet.[25]

Ahmed finds theoretical power in the term "intersectionality" to describe the positioning of women of color in a white supremacist, patriarchal, capitalist world; while Cooper finds Collin's matrix of domination more helpful in theorizing the place of women of color in the world and as feminists. Ahmed sets intersectional feminism against white feminism. White feminism is what Deborah King called "monistic": capable of capturing only one axis of domination, that of gender, as if it can be separated out from one's racial positioning. Intersectional feminism, as discussed earlier in this book, shows how each person's identities are constituted by multiple axes of dualist identities—Black/White, rich/poor, male/female, gay/straight, etc. Of course, none of these dualisms is "real" in the sense that no one person inhabits one side fully or successfully at all times. Intersectionality can be read like a metaphor that illuminates our complex structural and subjective relationships with the world. Ahmed is of Pakistani heritage. She grew up in England as a light-skinned brown girl who is now a brown-skinned queer woman.

Ahmed's writing puts on full display the tension between her desire to show feminism to be akin to the good life, the ethical life, and the right life and her commitment that living as a feminist is to be always questioning. "There is no guarantee that in struggling for justice we ourselves will be just." At times she is assertive: "To be a feminist at work is or should be about how we challenge everyday sexism . . . this is not optional. It is what makes feminism feminist."[26] Yet how do we "know" what everyday sexism is when we swim in the waters of a culture organized around gendered differences? How can we see outside of the normal?

This conundrum is pointed to in Ahmed's discussions about how important it is to make strange, to take some distance from, that which is familiar and normal if not always comfortable. For example, references to nature are common when describing the differences between men and women. Much of Ahmed's work is about "de-naturalizing" sexist assumptions about those differences. This is feminist work—it frees us from the normalizing language and gaze that control our behaviors, attitudes, and responses to sexist behavior.

Ahmed, commenting on her professional history as an academic philosopher, says "theory" is not hard. It is a language one moves around in, a set of ideas one becomes familiar enough with to write about independently, and a citational chain in which theorists respond to theorists and thus become theorists. This might come as a surprise to those struggling to understand obscure arguments. She says, however, explaining in various spaces of our lives that which is unthought, like gender dynamics, and thinking/acting to change are the more challenging, often gut-wrenching and life-changing tasks.[27] She suggests that harder than understanding complex theoretical texts is to expose injustices in the "texts" of everyday life that we take so much for granted, whether it be that girls are tomboys until they "grow up" or that "boys will be boys."

As an example of how we might act in this spirit of explaining the unthought habits of daily life, Ahmed unwinds these phrases that "explain" gendered behavior. She messes with "boys will be boys." "Will be" becomes a performative. Rather than "boys" being something prior to the enactment or description of boys, the phrase interpolates (calls into being) "boy" as an effect of a certain set of behaviors. Boys will be boys, or there will be consequences; therefore, boys are not just "being" boys—they are willed to be and must be willing to be boys. This way of reading, of seeing the multiple ways a single word could take on meanings that challenge normalized gendered/raced thinking, works its way all through Ahmed's text, showing what it is like to be a feminist, struggling to think otherwise than what we are habituated to think and, perhaps, mobilizing others to do the same. Another example is her reading of the phrase "sex assigned at birth." "Assignment" implies "homework," like one receives from school. To be at home in the world, one must do one's homework of being the sex assigned. The assignment is to be a sex. The sex does not exist prior to the assignment any more than school homework exists prior to being assigned as such. Thus, along with Judith Butler,[28] Ahmed says sex is something we do, not something we are. Her deconstruction of everyday phrases is feminism in action, not theory. If we hear words differently, we will see that what appears "normal" does not and perhaps should not have to be that way.

Staying close to the world means staying close to words, parsing their meanings and thus finding new ways of using them. Dismantling the master's house means radically deconstructing the master's tools, not using them as they were. These arguments guide Ahmed's thinking and writing.

Ahmed joins those individuals and movements that have reclaimed otherwise soul-crushing insults as emblems of pride, power, and collective joy. "Queer" is the best-known example. The word "queer," originally used by the British, referenced that which is "strange" or "off." As such, it was convenient to reference those indicating same-sex desire or who did not enact their "sex assignment at birth" in recognizable ("normal") ways. In the 1980s, lesbian, gay, bisexual, and trans groups began to self-identify as queer, to show how their existence in the world challenged norms and could lead in the libera-tory struggle around sex, sexuality, and gender identity.

Ahmed takes up the term "killjoy." It expresses for her what someone who calls out sexism and racism is doing from the per-spective of those for whom sexism or racism does not exist or for whom it is a preferred way of being in the world. She spends a lot of time with the feminist killjoy—retooling the common sensibility around what it is that "feminists do because they are feminists." The killjoy says something is sexist or racist and the room changes, the conversation shifts. They have created a problem—the problem that did not exist before they said something as a feminist. Feminists know/feel the problem did exist and name it, thus doing something with words. It is often called "interrupting," but interrupting implies once it is said everything can go on as normal once the interruption is over. This is not what happens when someone calls something racist or sexist. The scene shifts but rarely in recognition that the killjoy is correct, rarely in the direction of reflective discussion of what happened. People in the room will go on the offensive or defensive but seldom acknowledge and reflect together on what happened.

Her approach through the figure of the feminist killjoy is to empower individuals to name the dynamics that are somewhat pre-dictable when they speak up or "act out." Whether it is the mother who refuses the default caretaker position in a family; the worker who protests the pornographic calendars; the professional caretaker who insists on eight-hour shifts, a regular schedule, and decent pay and benefits; the colleague in a meeting who calls out racist com-ments; or the daughter at the dinner table (Ahmed's experience) who calls out family members for sexism—all are disrupting what otherwise will be identified as labors of love and care, trivial, or "merely" politically incorrect behavior.

Ahmed presents the figure of the lesbian as the ultimate killjoy of patriarchal/masculinist orders. Her chapter on lesbian-feminism reaches back to political groups, manifestos, and literature that theorize lesbian desire as a refusal to devote one's time to satisfying the masculinist gaze or the professed needs of male partners. It is not only refusal, however; it is also joyful. She quotes a classic novel by Rita Mae Brown titled *Rubyfruit Jungle*. A student is confronted by the Dean of her college about her relationship with her female roommate:

> Dean: Is this relationship with Faye Raider of an, uh—intimate nature?
> Student: We fuck, if that's what you're after.
> *I think her womb collapsed on that one. Sputtering, she pressed forward.*
> Dean: Don't you find that somewhat of an aberration? Doesn't this disturb you, my dear? After all, it's not normal.
> Student: I know it's not normal for people in this world to be happy, and I'm happy.[29]

In being the killjoy, the student finds her joy. This is not often what happens when we speak up, since we each exist in different contexts and are navigating different conditions; but for Ahmed, the essential point is made in the student's rejoinder. The student leaves the word "normal" on the table for assessment rather than accepting the authoritative or habitual meaning expressed by the Dean. Normative heterosexuality is not what everyone wants and certainly not what everyone needs to be happy. Complying with the demand, though it is not fulfilling one's desire, feeds the machine of patriarchy and affirms masculinity as always getting what it wants.

I use the phrase "the figure of the lesbian" because Ahmed is theorizing the meaning and significance of queerness among self-identified women, not articulating a demand for each individual woman to live up to. She never says one need be a lesbian to be a feminist. Rather, she is interpreting the effects of queerness on a system. Many lesbian women will follow the patterns and models of heterosexual patriarchal capitalist culture in getting married (requesting the imprimatur of the patriarchal state), aspiring to a middle-class lifestyle (accommodating capitalist norms of success), and creating nuclear, privatized spaces for their familial form. This is not addressed in

Ahmed's chapter; she is theorizing a politics of withdrawal from and the creation of alternative spaces of intimacy and potential political action. She wants to reclaim radical feminism from the critics who say it sets out our options as either withdrawal from *or* accommodation to oppressive structures.

At the end of her book, Ahmed offers a feminist killjoy handbook and a manifesto. She recommends those willing to take up the role of feminist killjoy have certain things: books, spaces, friends, activities, and exit plans. She also, interestingly, appends a "Feminist Killjoy Manifesto" to her book. As is her style in the rest of the book, which reads like a manifesto, she is making manifest what she has argued throughout a feminist killjoy to be taking on and why. Manifestos are simultaneously critiques of what is imposed as normal and necessary in life (capitalist relations of production or, in this case, heteronormative sexuality) and visionary statements. In calling out sexism, sexist exploitation, and sexist oppression as they intertwine with racism, racist exploitation, and racist oppression, and joining in the reclamation of queerness as the ultimate "calling out," she is acting through writing. Her purpose is one of persuasion, but also of mobilization. She builds an argument deploying a tone and style of assertion, even while one assertion she makes in the beginning is that feminism must remain open to its own shortcomings and each feminist must remain vulnerable to critique.

Ahmed identifies a central paradox of feminism: that we continue to have to argue the existence of the problems feminisms struggle to define and resolve. From the speak-outs of the 1970s to the #MeToo movement of the late 2010s, massive numbers of women, millions of stories, persistent repetition, are necessary simply to persuade the public that a problem (reproductive life and death, gendered socio-economic deprivation, sexual assault) is indeed a problem. Those speaking out, persistently attempting to politicize the personal, lack credibility. An example: until the 1970s, courts required male witnesses to testify before giving credence to women's claims of sexual assault. Have things changed if millions of stories are still required to corroborate the claim that sexual assault is a systematic social/political problem? This is the case to varying degrees with all forms of oppression. The case must continually be made that there is a problem in the first place.

NIVEDITA MENON, *SEEING LIKE A FEMINIST*[30]

Nivedita Menon's work weaves together policy discussions and feminist critique, ascertaining when and how different feminisms have produced certain kinds of knowledge about gender, women, and femininity. Menon engages with Indian history and contemporary policy, considering the complex intersections of caste, regional differences, religious sectarianism, and neocolonial capitalism with what is argued to "be good for women." Her book offers a wide range of challenges and insights while placing markers along the way as to what she argues feminism itself should be.

Menon takes on several policy areas that have taken center stage in Indian politics with respect to gendered traditions and laws, showing how "seeing like a feminist" can help us measure the extent to which they benefit or disadvantage the many intersecting identities that constitute the deeply fissured Indian "public." She highlights debates among Indian feminists about policy, and how some approaches collude with conservative morality-based arguments about properly gendered prerogative, behavior, and public or private comportment. "Seeing like a feminist" gathers meaning as we read Menon's book and consider her conclusions.

Menon argues throughout that feminists should not assume "woman" as an embodied identity subsuming all other aspects of their existence in various communities. The binary man/woman as definitive of gender identity has been shown not to be universal; rather, it is specific to Western histories and the colonial imagination as to how communities express gendered existence. Further, the bias toward assuming one is studying "women" because one's subjects of research appear, through Western presumptions about gender as an embodied "fact", as women performing roles within the social/economic order reproduces the idea that gender identity is preordained while other identities are "added on." Menon references groundbreaking work by Oyeronke Oyewumi as an example of what Menon means by "seeing like a feminist." Oyewumi criticizes researchers who study "women in Africa" as if being "women" is a preordained reality upon which "roles" are layered. Oyewumi criticizes research, for example, that identifies as market women those persons who are Yoruban traders. This assumes they are first women who happen to be traders. However, in Ghana, trader was the primary marker of identity, not gender. Hence the researcher, seeking women, found traders.[31] "Seeing like a feminist" need not assume the category "woman" in advance but will do better to understand that the biological determinism established in the West over the last 500 years is not universal; rather, it has been universalized by way of colonization and consequent epistemic domination, meaning it is how we know the truth about our own and other's gender identities.

In focusing on Indian politics, Menon's book argues the impossibility of creating a nationalized policy that can take into account the very different ways people identified as women have influence or are subordinated by communal habits and beliefs. Simultaneously, it becomes clear that standardizing women's conditions within the multifaceted traditions of various religious and communal identities in India is central to the identity of the land mass in the South Asian continent as India. This case study of India shows that if we assume gender as an embodied experience prior to all else, we will seek to establish standardizing policies that may undo the radically different dynamics, gendered or otherwise, already in place that serve those identified as women better. There is no such thing as "the Indian woman" whose wellbeing will be addressed by laws passed at the national level. Muslim, Dalit, urban, secular, Hindi, and subsistence farmers who are also identified as female will not receive benefits or disadvantages in the same way as "women."

For example, Menon shows how individualizing property rights (alienation) suborns some women's status in communities that had communal rights. In a patriarchal society, alienation of property through testamentary wills individualizes property holdings, making it more available to capture by capitalist and state interests, whether men or women possess it as individuals. Further, daughters in communal property arrangements were guaranteed to be taken care of because the property could not be alienated except by the (unlikely) agreement of the community. The state moved to individualize property holdings, to render ownership more "transparent" than it is under "traditional" communal title. Under the new privatized property regime, women had the right to own property; but fathers—as they no longer had the communally supported obligation to share property with women in their family—could then use property as a cudgel, threatening disinheritance to disempower daughters. The loopholes that would prevent women from owning property reassured those patriarchal outcomes of property rights beyond thinking in abstract terms of how individual women might benefit. Women and men are embedded in various historical contexts which shape the outcomes of policy beyond whether it serves individuals. Menon shows that there is nothing "natural" about arrangements of family under color of law in India, and that the modernizing discourse of rights may or may not serve those identified as women within the vastly different contexts of religious, caste, or regional differences.

Menon reveals us how seeing like a feminist is also a critique of the national project of India; the standardization of policy across differences may or may not advantage women; and most certainly, any discourse of "modernization" is suspect when capitalist and patriarchal interests are intertwined in the discourse legitimating the policy. Feminists thus must pay attention to more than the abstract "rights" of women being articulated in modernization discourse.

On questions related to desire and love and sexuality, Menon identifies queer identities as those which threaten heteronormativity, also referred to as compulsory heterosexuality. She makes claims and asks questions that demand further consideration—which is what feminism, as such, typically does (we do not settle our own debates easily!). In India, she argues, the catastrophe of the HIV-AIDS epidemic in the 1980s and 1990s rendered it possible for sexuality to "come out of the closet" under cover, so to speak, of discussing a deadly disease understood to be spread by sexual contact. Seeing like a feminist clarifies the relationship between the catastrophe of HIV-AIDS and the subsequent movement for LGBTQIA+ rights.

Menon states her case about feminism most clearly in a chapter titled "Feminists and Women." She says feminism is not about women. It is about "recognizing how modern discourses produce human beings who are exclusively 'men' or 'women.'"[32] She goes on to assert that feminism is not just about gender. It must "see" the intersections with caste, religion, work, queer, and/or regional location alongside the unending ways in which meaning is produced and gender is experienced. Menon's articulation of what feminism is about is not original to her. She is drawing on many feminist theorists, some of whom would be surprised to see their names in her book. However, her title "seeing like a feminist" captures the significance of these ideas about feminism because she argues feminism interprets the nuances, the ethical dilemmas, and the conflicts over outcomes among advocates with respect to policies that have material and long-term impacts on the quality of our gendered existence.

Menon's work focuses our attention on the political economies of gendered structures and other deeply ingrained demands on individuals to organize themselves as subjects and as citizens in particular ways, the primary one being the "family." She has in common with early feminists not an abolitionist perspective on family, but a critique that puts the political economies of family and the changes wrought by colonialist dynamics at the center of analysis.

VERONICA GAGO, *THE FEMINIST INTERNATIONAL: HOW TO CHANGE EVERYTHING*[33]

Veronica Gago is an Argentine feminist thinker and organizer. This book offers wide-ranging yet deeply interconnected analyses of the work feminisms could and should be doing. Gago's purpose is to argue about and for the feminist *strike* as a site of networked and connected political resistance and prefigurative models for living a more just life together. Her title communicates an unwieldy ambition. It may be read as a rhetorical flourish to capture the imaginations of those who feel small and helpless in the face of a dauntingly damaged world and a description of the scope of the analysis she carries out in the book. She articulates the possibilities in the feminist strike to force thinking about why and how everything needs changing and how mass mobilizations across multiple sectors of society hold the possibilities of change.

In the US, in the 1970s, feminists emphasized remaking relationships among women through feminism. Feminist consciousness-raising and mobilization would generate forms of woman-identified political, social, and economic analysis and woman-identified activism and solidarity. Feminism would inspire women to act in their interests as a class, radically subverting/overcoming patriarchal dominance and male-identified structures of power. Feminist mobilization would inspire women's liberation. The sisterhood model of feminism—that the sex-gender system is women's primary shared lived experience—was, however, driven by white, middle-class feminists. The upshot of criticisms leveled at white feminists is that they projected their lived experiences as those that define the oppression of all women in relationship to all men. Universalizing discourses of global sisterhood are a recognizable feminist ideal that developed traction across the globe but was unsustainable. Over a short time, feminist activists and thinkers broke down the "shared experience" model and showed that we must deeply consider context; race, class, sexuality, and geographic location matter.

The feminism that asserts that women as such have needs, desires, and interests that, to be fulfilled, require the end of male dominance and oppression remains a powerful organizing discourse for analysis and activity. The "end of male dominance and oppression" has not been accomplished, but organized efforts in the name of women and girls have deepened and become institutionalized. Globally, there are women's policy agencies and state-sponsored organizations that focus on girls and women and drive initiatives to change the lives of women for the better. These organizations that call for the empowerment of women and girls, as noted throughout this book, sometimes identify as feminist, sometimes not, but few explicitly identify the problem as male dominance. Strategies focus on distributing resources, legislating reforms, and bureaucratic policy prescriptions. Much of it is inspired by the sense that states can identify as "modern" through a less obviously oppressive treatment of women, while sustaining traditional reproductive and household and familial norms. If we "see like feminists," as Menon suggests, we will see that state-sponsored reform does not capture the heterogeneous needs and desires of those identified as women and girls. Or, as Banet-Weisser argues, state actors and policymakers will focus on neoliberal versions of individualized initiative without changing the deeply entrenched expectations of gendered life or the radically unequal profit-oriented distribution of material resources.

Veronica Gago's title, *Feminist International: How to Change Everything*, itself is a provocation to make connections among the myriads of systematic injustices that plague late modernity. Her book conceptualizes the feminist strike: it is an analysis of the motivating elements of neoliberalism; a compendium of connections among movements already mobilized in communities; and, importantly, a radical rethinking of what constitutes work, labor, participation, and contribution to the public and social good.

In October 2016, in Argentina, feminists mobilized massive street demonstrations under the banner *"Ni una Menos."* This was a reaction to the murder of Lucia Perez, a young woman killed and then impaled by her boyfriend because she would not have an abortion. The men involved in her torture and death were convicted of drug crimes. The court dismissed the rape and murder charges on the grounds that they could not establish whether "consent" was involved. The street mobilizations were triggered by this absurd conclusion and grew into a general strike to protest the increase in femicides across the country and violence against women generally. The men responsible for Perez's torture and death were not convicted of that crime until 2023, after enormous national pressure was brought to bear on the court to recognize the gendered/sexualized violence committed against her.

Gago explains the size and power of the history-making feminist strikes that followed in the wake of the 2016 mobilization and spread across the world as possible because of long-term organizing among women in Argentina. In Argentina, feminists have been organizing annual National Women's Encuentros since 1986. In the US, there was one such assembly in 1976, discussed in Chapter 2. Since 1986, the Argentine meeting has changed its call to a "Plurinational Encuentro of Women, Lesbians, Travestis, Trans and Non-Binary People."[34] It has decentered "woman" as definitive of feminism or of the politics of gender. Gago also attributes the successful street mobilizations to the historical tradition of popular mobilization dating back to the violently repressive military dictatorship of the 1970s. Street mobilizations by popular organizations are not sporadic in Argentina; they are an integral part of doing politics. "Popular" here is not defined as "well liked" or in terms of a successful marketing strategy. It reflects an emphasis on mobilizing from the ground up, from communities and the lived experiences of ordinary people. It counters the tendency of states to coopt the organizing energies and capacities of communities experiencing oppressive cultural and material conditions into technocratic solutions that reach only a few and fail to undo the systems that create the problems in the first place.

The feminist strike, as assessed by Gago, moves to connect the movements of an otherwise sectarian popular sphere. Since 2016, the feminist strike, held on International Women's Day, March 8, has mobilized across Latin America and Europe. But why a "strike" in particular?

Conceptualized in the broadest sense, the strike is a stoppage of activity. Reflecting labor history, it has typically referred to labor actions in the formal, legal economy. When workers strike, they withhold labor, their ultimate lever in the power struggle against the companies and bosses that run them. In Argentina, there was resistance by the labor movements about whether the "strike" could be appropriated for non-union identified movements. Gago and the organizers of the feminist strikes starting in 2016 argue that unions do not represent all who labor; nor should the strike be considered the tool only of waged laborers. Gago's book follows in a long feminist tradition of critique of traditional Marxist and socialist thinking that leaves reproductive labor and domestic relationships in the shadows until the labor force has, in its evolution, rendered all people workers as a class in opposition to capital. The feminist strike argues that the "private space," as created by liberal capitalism to be the space of reproduction and as a result the space of non-productivity, is anachronistic. Women are wage workers even while they do the work of the home and the community, making possible the conditions that reproduce capital. All communities should be included in those who strike, whether they are in the informal or formal economy. In Gago's telling, the inclusive quality of the 21st century strike challenges the notion that there are factions of oppressed peoples that join up every so often against a common enemy. Rather, she relates the strike as a process, not an event; it does not assume the connections among the oppressed as such. It knows those connections must be actively made and worked on. The strike gives time, Gago argues, for the assemblies involved to process connections and be involved in a process of protest and of building alternatives to the status quo. It is the assemblies that create the terms for the strike, not the strike that gives voice to the assemblies. This is a model of decentralization used by the global Occupy Movements in 2011–2012 and by other anti-globalization movements of the 21st century. However, the feminist strike organizes, gives a space for multitudes to see one another as they make connections otherwise unseen by traditional forms of "interest group" or "social movement" mobilizations.

The feminist strike organizers use the term "transversal." According to Gago, this is a way of articulating connections—for example, that all women and feminized figures are always already workers creating value. The strike cannot remain the domain of unions as representative of workers. This carries the potential of linking violence against women with barriers to and conditions of work in the informal and formal economy. It makes visible the way financialization (debt) produces the promise of future indentured labor by those who rely on credit to provide support for everyday life as austerity policies diminish access to resources. The stripping of autonomy from community kitchens and the incorporation of food aid into the formal and distant mechanisms of the state transversalize kitchen workers as they are displaced as workers in the community space. This term works to critique and defy the production of sectoral differences in the popular space.

Gago's call for a radically different abortion politics clarifies how the feminist strike shifts the discourse of abortion from one of "instrumental need" or "individual rights" to one of desire. Abortion is described here not as an instrumental means to another end of either economic wellbeing or choice, but rather as a mode of desire. Desire should not be obscured by a language of "choice" as if it is a purely instrumental act to be or not be a mother. Desire, or lack thereof, to be a parent is a part of our lived experience and must speak its name in social movements for autonomy. While desire might sound self-serving and self-indulgent to some ears, feminisms have always argued for the freeing of women to enact their desiring selves, out from under the demand for procreational service and/or patriarchal constructions of sexuality and sex. This is not about the "Truth" of what "women" want. Thinking in terms of desire is to shift from thinking about "choice," which relegates the decision to a rationalist accounting process, a kind of cost/benefit assessment. Desire is more ephemeral and identifies conditions in which we want to live, not a "choice" based on individual preference or necessity. Material conditions and public expectations of what mothers are supposed to be and do are oppressive. If conditions radically changed, we don't know what the outcome would be. We should change the conditions because it is the right thing to do and see what happens without telling women, "We will fund childcare because it will lead to fewer abortions." Transactional discourse diminishes the value of the desiring self.

The chapter on sexual violence—or what has commonly been referred to as the "war on women," given the levels of femicide across the globe—highlights Gago's sensibilities about the interconnectedness of otherwise siloed issues and identities. She traces what is new in feminist critiques of sexualized violence, showing that the pluralization of the forms this violence takes does not just categorize harms and does not concern itself with establishing cause and effect, as if there is an origin to sexual violence which, if we could ferret it out and eliminate it, would result in an end to sexual violence. Rather, she speaks of "transversality," of the way the strike enacts and produces meaning throughout the network of forms of exploitation and dispossession of those participating. Sexual violence is not a harm among other harms. It is a constitutive experience and attaches to environmental conditions that financialization and capitalism create which simultaneously require radical change.

Gago, in her assessment of the feminist strike, persistently undoes "dualisms" or contrasts that separate the local/regional from the global/hegemonic forces. For example, the US and Europe, sometimes referred to as the "Global North," are centers of finance capital, a non-productive means by which capital builds without producing material stuff. Latin America and the "Global south" are identified as sites of continuing extraction of raw materials and labor to sustain the global machine of production. This idea that finance is not productive fails to see how it produces debt, it produces demand through data analysis, and it finances mega-extractive systems of production. Feminists do not typically attend to issues of finance capital except as an afterthought when discussing women in marginalized and precarious conditions. Gago insists feminists must "see" finance and the impact of this abstract force on how we live and make things in the world. Finance capital, such as that wielded by private equity firms, takes things—spaces of life and production—and turns them into data-informed machines of extraction. Venture capital is extractive of value in the businesses that must show, in advance through a "pitch," that they will serve a market, a need, a space of innovation.

The feminism Gago describes and argues for in *Feminist International* is constructed by way of popular assemblies. Feminism is the scaffolding upon which popular resistance and change will be built, but it is not built in the same way in any two different moments or places. The popular assembly differs from the consciousness-raising strategies of feminisms described earlier in this book. The popular assembly is specifically organized around seeking connections among issues brought to the space. How is femicide connected to labor and finance and neoliberal rationalities? Where are sex workers in the systems that oppress all workers? How do reproductive policies restrict and diminish women in general? To what use are repressive reproductive policies put in the neoliberal project of privatization and individuation? How does the assembly avoid traps of particularized victimization and generate, across movements, organizations and desires, actions against the diverse strategies of neoliberalism? Since 2016, when femicide was the primary kind of violence resisted by the feminist strike in October, the strike extended over space and time and movements. Gago argues that the feminist strike makes space for popular contestation about the world as it is and the world that we want.

This idea of "the popular" is not the commodification or signaling of feminism that Banet-Weisser describes. The "popular" in Latin American politics does not reference that which individuals prefer. Popular movements are organized by marginal and oppressed peoples and identify their aspirations with the common good, not with interests or sectarian demands. The popular assembly is inclusive, but not in the neoliberal sense of allowing many kinds of individuals to participate in projects already formed by way statist or capitalist interests. Rather, the popular assembly creates the commons as it goes and identifies how the commons can be a space of securing life and freedom for everyone. A popular feminism thus makes connections through practice and action.

I chose to close this chapter with Veronica Gago's book as it offers analyses and demands that amplify feminism as a force in the world. How these demands are articulated differs from the ways feminists have attempted to bring women into feminism as "woman." All issues associated with injustice, inequality, and human suffering are feminist issues, only in part because those who identify as women and are identified as such experience these harms disproportionately. This does not mean women or feminists are responsible for saving the world. This means that feminist analysis and action are necessary for everything from the debt crisis to mass incarceration to childcare to hunger. It is feminist argument that will make the connections and draw out the networks. These are feminist issues because these harms have fallen on and been assumed to be the work of women to manage. Further, with Gago, we can identify historical "correlations." While we might focus on evidence as to cause and effect, it remains a fact that as more women are in college in the US, for example, the finance systems that produce and thrive on indebtedness have crippled higher education. Private equity firms acquire industries that employ mostly women and care for the most vulnerable among us—nursing homes and childcare centers—extracting value from women's labor. When austerity measures squeeze already suffering communities, violence and competition for resources play out against women as mothers, wives, and daughters. Independence for women becomes more difficult as the work they do includes the unpaid care work alongside the waged work that leaves families and communities under-resourced and in need. Private industry and states take land that does not belong to them. This displaces the indigenous communities that have sustained those spaces by means unrecognizable within systems that only value certain kinds of productivity and outcomes from human activity.

Feminism is in and of all these dynamics as a way of knowing, or "seeing" as Nivedita Menon says. Feminism for Gago is not about saving or uplifting or empowering women. It is about confronting and challenging all structures of oppression that are sexist (as bell hooks tells us), but always more than sexist as we think about how we want to live in the world. To link feminism to sexism and sexist oppression is not enough. The linkages must expand and grow and change as circumstances and strategies of oppression change. This is what Gago argues *Feminist International* is about. It is not about women as a class with the same interests in overcoming male dominance. It is about how structures of oppression and exploitation undo the lives we live as gendered persons. It is material and cultural. It is about the networks and connections that impact and change lives for the better or for the worse and figuring out the difference through assembly, active resistance, and the creation of alternatives.

CONCLUSION

None of the books I discuss here references "waves" or any other linear progression of feminism. Persuasive critiques of that approach to classifying feminisms have encouraged thinkers and activists to engage with the complexity and specificity of feminist writing, theory, and practices rather than classifying them as old or new or better or worse. Sara Ahmed reaches back to radical and lesbian-feminist writing from the 1970s that many dismiss as too proscriptive or narrow in its thinking about gender dynamics. She reminds us of the power of lesbian desire as a subversive challenge to patriarchal dominance and control. She highlights the joy of the separatist impulse among women to get out from under the male gaze even while they risked everything to do so. Brittney Cooper reaches back to Black Feminists who were aware of the injustice of the demand that formerly enslaved people assimilate to white bourgeois norms. The gatekeepers of privilege were former masters. White supremacy shapes Black lives and confronting that through eloquent rage, asserting desire, and refusing respectability while demanding respect are her strategies for living a Black Feminist life. Nivedita Menon references feminist work from all over the world to build the scaffolding to see like a feminist. She references the contributions of feminist theorists of male dominance from the US and feminist critiques of Western imperial feminisms. Breaking down the category "woman" to find those identified and who identify as women and girls and traders and family members and workers in all their complexity is to see like a feminist. Veronica Gago tells us that we must break what we think to be feminism into its multitudinous possibilities and recognize its potential to end oppressive processes and projects while building something new. A global feminism is not a universalizing feminism; it is a transversal feminism.

NOTES

1 Banet-Weisser Sarah, *Empowered: Popular Feminism and Popular Misogyny* (Duke University Press, 2018).
2 Klein, Naomi, *No Logo* (Picador Press, 2009).
3 Jay-Z raps, "I'm not a businessman, I'm a business, man" on Kanye West's "Diamonds from Sierra Leone (Remix)" (2005).
4 Cooper, Brittney *Eloquent Rage: A Black Feminist Discovers Her Superpower* (St. Martins Press, 2018) 121.
5 Cooper, ibid.
6 Cooper, ibid 121
7 Cooper, Brittney *Beyond Respectability: The Intellectual Thought of Race Women* (University of Illinois Press, 2017).

8 Cooper, ibid 141

9 Cooper, ibid 147

10 Cooper, Brittney C., Susana M. Morris, and Robin M. Boylorn (eds.), *The Crunk Feminist Collection* (The Feminist Press at CUNY, 2016).

11 Cooper et al., ibid 4.

12 Morgan, Joan, *When Chickenheads Come Home to Roost: A Hip-Hop Feminist Breaks it Down* (Simon and Schuster, 2000).

13 Cooper, ibid 90.

14 Morgan, ibid.

15 hooks, bell, *We Real Cool: Black Men and Masculinity* (Routledge, 2004).

16 Morgan, ibid 39.

17 Morgan, ibid 40.

18 Collins, Patricia Hill, *Black Feminist Thought: Knowledge, Consciousness, and the Politics of Empowerment* (Routledge, 1990).

19 Morgan uses this phrase repeatedly in *Chickenheads*.

20 Cooper et al., ibid 11.

21 Traister, Rebecca, *Good and Mad: The Revolutionary Power of Women's Anger* (Simon and Schuster, 2018).

22 Ahmed, Sara, *Living a Feminist Life* (Duke University Press, 2016).

23 Ahmed, ibid 4.

24 Ahmed, ibid 234

25 Ahmed, ibid14

26 Ahmed, ibid 6

27 Ahmed, ibid 8

28 Butler, Judith, *Gender Trouble* (Routledge, 1990).

29 Brown, Rita Mae, *Rubyfruit Jungle* (Random House, 2015).

30 Menon, Nivedita, *Seeing Like a Feminist* (India Penguin, 2012).

31 Oyewumi, Oyewunke, *The Invention of Woman: An African Sense of Western Gender Discourse* (University of Minnesota Press, 2007), cited in Menon, ibid 54.

32 Menon, ibid 149.

33 Gago, Veronica, *The Feminist International: How to Change Everything* (Verso, 2020).

34 The 36th women's meeting is described by one of the participants, South Feminist Futures, at https://southfeministfutures.org/36th-plurinational-encounter-of-women-lesbians-transvestites-trans-bisexuals-intersexuals-and-non-binaries-2023/.

6

CONCLUSION

Contemporary authoritarianism is identified with versions of masculinity that are presented publicly through ritualistic displays of dominance and impunity, and that are deadly for millions of people. This might be evidence that, globally, feminism is on the wane or on the defensive. However, we should also recognize that the sensationalist and scandal-ridden Trumpism, the absurdly masculinist performances of Vladimir Putin, the male chauvinist antics of Boris Johnson in England, the explicit and targeted violence of the Proud Boys in the US, reflect—like prisms reflect splinters of light—the historical impacts of feminisms. Contemporary masculinist reactions are dangerous, driven by hyperbolic, irrational fears about the loss of masculine prerogative, privilege, and control. However, the reactive rhetorics and dangerous actions and policies are being enacted on shaky ground that will not stabilize.

In much (not all) of human history, males dominated in the public and private spaces of life. If we take a longer view than this description of our contemporary condition suggests, in a short 100 years, feminisms have destabilized patriarchy. Gendered and sexed existence will never again settle into any of the kinds of patriarchal equilibrium argued for by contemporary authoritarian leaders and self-identified "male chauvinist" militias. Feminist perspectives have been institutionalized at the international level through the auspices of the United Nations; in the Rome Treaty governing the International Criminal Court, which defines rape as a war crime; and in progress made in Ireland, Mexico, Argentina, and many other seemingly intractable patriarchal cultures on abortion rights. The impact of feminist work is seen in the numbers of

DOI: 10.4324/9781003264682-6

non-cisgendered, non-male, non-heterosexual, and non-white people in all branches of government and levels of governance worldwide. Women's rights are part of the conversation. Further, the heterosexist binary governing gender identity is scrambling to defend itself. Donald Trump felt it necessary to issue an executive order stating (falsely) that there are two sexes and therefore two genders, and that all federal policy shall respect those "facts" in the name of protecting women.[1] This explicit command that an otherwise naturalized binary must be defended indicates that how we understand sex and gender will never again be taken for granted. The executive order is symptomatic of the thorough politicization of what had been thought to be true. The complexity and injustices of binary gender identity imperatives cannot be unseen by the public. That people called "women" must be protected by people called "men" resonates with some, but they cannot unsee the challenges and are having to explicitly and vociferously defend their ground.

In short, patriarchy, white supremacy, and presumptions about the meaning of gender and sexed identities are on the table and will not be cleared off. What could be assumed about femininity and masculinity as defined against each other now must be argued for, written into legislation, and publicly defended. While that has always been the case to some degree, it is now part of the global political cultural and policy apparatuses that shape lives. This is not a silver lining analysis. Reactions against threat to masculinist prerogatives are violent and those reacting remain dominant forces in most societies. This is to say that there has been a tectonic shift that will never shift back into anything like what those reacting are calling for. We can look at the 4B movement in South Korea for an excellent example of how feminists' resistance is infusing the social order with new kinds of conflicts over norms and habits associated with gendered and sexed imperatives.[2]

I have not discussed feminist fiction in this book. It is, obviously, critical to feminisms' contemporary ubiquity in culture and in political spaces. Two iconic representations of imagined futures illustrate the hopes and fears of feminists over the last five decades of feminist work. Marge Piercy wrote *Woman on the Edge of Time* in 1976.[3] Margaret Atwood wrote *The Handmaid's Tale* in 1985.[4] The latter became a renowned streaming series discussed across the world, distributed first in 2017 (coinciding with the #MeToo movement).

Woman on the Edge of Time follows Consuela, a Puerto Rican-American woman living in New York in the 1970s. However, when she faces traumatic incidents in her present, she is transported to a gender-utopic community of the future called Mattapoisett. This future holds no space for gender. The only pronoun is "per." Sex is egalitarian and erotic. There is respect for privacy, but it is not grounded in spatial arrangements like homes and/or the economy, and it is not linked to femininity and masculinity enacted in terms of private and public activities. It is respected for the value of being apart from the social space and/or solitude for wellbeing. Freedom is founded in the contingent rather than foundational qualities of identity and desire. Characters and personalities are complicated and well developed as part of the storyline, but conflicts are not attached to ownership—either of those one loves, or of property, or in prerogative. Influence is wielded by way of experience, age, respect, and the capacity to listen and respond, not by way of demand or reaction. Rituals take the form of games and, often, erotic engagements, not the pomp and circumstance performed as legitimation ceremonies for the powerful. Spirituality permeates the lived experience and atmosphere of the community but not institutionalized religion.

Piercy's story is meant to contrast this non-gendered-sexed environment with Consuela's present life as the aunt of a young woman viciously abused by a pimp. Connie is locked into an asylum because she fights back against the violence inflicted in the private, gendered space of the small apartment she calls home. The "present" is mostly defined by her struggle for survival in the asylum and her battle against a masculinist medical profession determined to "normalize" her. Utopia in Piercy's book is the absence of binary gender norms and the policing of sexuality, not "blindness" to gender and the privacy of sexuality.

Atwood's *The Handmaid's Tale* shows the opposite future in a swath of territory in the US transformed into a society named Gilead. In Gilead, gender-sexed difference has become the organizing principle of human relationships. Men are men together as dominant figures and women are women together as subordinate figures.

Men, as commanders, decide all public affairs and arrangements. Some women, called handmaids, are vessels of ritualized reproduction made possible by ritualized rape. Other women, married to commanders, are appointed a handmaid who will serve as the vessel to produce a child for the commander's family to raise. Among the protagonists of the book is a woman, married to a commander, who has been an intellectual and charismatic force in creating this new society. The story is told about and through the perspective of her handmaid. In Gilead, any visible sign of dissent is punished by torturous death with bodies displayed publicly on a wall along a public pathway. Women not suited to marriage or capable of reproduction are sent to the colonies to clean up toxic waste that presumably created the environmental disaster leading to the infertility "crisis" that inspired Gilead.

In this tale, slavery is founded in gender, sex, and reproductive capacities, not the capacity to labor. Black women who were enslaved experienced all the above for 400 years; in Gilead, it is the fate of all fertile women as women. Women are divided up depending upon whether they are fertile. The non-fertile women are divided up depending upon whether they should be used as wives, housemaids, or sex objects. Rape is a publicly sanctioned and ritualized means by which to create another generation rather than a privately held prerogative of slave masters or husbands. *The Handmaid's Tale* is a book about resistance against totalitarian control of bodies and minds. We do not know from the book whether June—the handmaid who flees—manages to escape, whether she survives, or whether she leads a revolution. There is no conclusive or cathartic moment that ends the nightmare.

These novels narrate the endgame implicit in the patriarchal compulsion to control women's bodies. Women are reduced to their reproductive and nurturing selves, by way of totalitarian governance; violence and social neurosis are the result. The stories and descriptions of Mattapoisett in *Woman on the Edge of Time* are capacious in envisioning what life could be without any gendered, racial, or class arrangements. Identity in Mattapoisett, as witnessed by Consuela, is contingent; it is experienced in the moment, not inhabited over time, and given grace for its peculiarities and idiosyncrasies as it is expressed in the world. It shows we do not require static versions of identity to cultivate personality and differences and conflict and resolution. Our psychic interiority can be more experimental and, while not unbound (there are rules and rituals), freer.

The Handmaid's Tale tells the story of what happens when the gender binary is policed more rigidly for whatever reason—whether that be theocratic, pragmatic (birthrates), or because masculinity requires the binary as its defining arrangement to remain dominant.

Each reflects many of the principles and arguments described in this book. Neither novel captures how feminisms are living on and developing, in all their many versions, today. Nor do they exhaust how we might imagine a future organized otherwise than this one, with its dangerous reliance on axes of difference that map onto relationships of dominance and subordination. They do, however, capture the spirit of feminisms as inventive, experimental, and exploratory.

Feminisms are not for everyone. Feminisms are critiques of unjust systems, norms, laws, and policies—at least they will be until a different future beyond dominance and subordination emerges. Because we have no way of knowing if or when that future could emerge, and because we can see only glimpses of it given present circumstances, feminisms are arguments about what is and what should be. Because they are arguments, there will be disagreement. In fact, feminisms will no longer be necessary in a feminist future. We should note that there are no feminists in Mattapoisett.

This book is designed to offer a glimpse of what feminisms as world-building claims, and arguments, and visionary critiques offer. Claiming affinity with feminisms of any sort is a necessarily political act and therefore difficult. It generates controversy. As Ahmed says, in stating a problem, feminism becomes a problem. That said, I think that feminisms do not require "identification." Rather, feminisms emerge with a willingness to see differently (shift perspectives), argue (make political claims), and consistently resist policies that follow from the policing necessary for any version of identity that requires a dominant and subordinate form to remain in place. It is an act of rhetorical defiance to claim feminism for one's own. That said, the feminism one claims has no more essential truth to it than does the patriarchal culture from which it emerges and to which it responds. It lives on and develops in the plural, as arguments among other arguments for what must be different if justice is to be realized.

NOTES

1 White House, "Defending Women from Gender Ideology Extremism and Restoring Biological Truth to the Federal Government," January 20, 2025. https://www.whitehouse.gov/presidential-actions/2025/01/defending-women-from-gender-ideology-extremism-and-restoring-biological-truth-to-the-federal-government/

2 Gao, Ming, " 'A Woman is Not a Baby-Making Machine: A Brief History of South Korea's 4B Movement and Why It's Making Waves in America," *The Conversation*, November 11, 2024. https://theconversation.com/a-woman-is-not-a-baby-making-machine-a-brief-history-of-south-koreas-4b-movement-and-why-its-making-waves-in-america-243355

3 Piercy, Marge, *Woman on the Edge of Time* (Alfred A. Knopf, 1976).

4 Atwood, Margaret, *The Handmaid's Tale* (Houghton-Mifflin, 1985).

BIBLIOGRAPHY

Allen, Pam, *Free Space: A Perspective on the Small Group in Women's Liberation* (Times Change Press, 2000).

Barnard Center for Research on Women, "Wages for Housework" flyer. https://bcrw.barnard.edu/archive/workforce/Wages_for_Housework.pdf

Brennan, Teresa and Carol Pateman "Mere Auxiliaries to the Commonwealth: Women and the Origins of Liberalism" *Political Studies* 27 2 (1979).

Butler, Judith, *Gender Trouble: Feminism and the Subversion of Identity* (Routledge, 1990).

Butler, Judith, "Imitation and Gender Insubordination" in Henry Abelove (ed.) *The Lesbian and Gay Reader* (Routledge, 1993).

Collins, Patricia Hill, *Black Feminist Thought: Knowledge, Consciousness, and the Politics of Empowerment* (Routledge, 2008).

Collins, Patricia Hill, *Intersectionality as Critical Social Theory* (Duke University Press, 2019).

Cooper, Christine, "Worrying about Vaginas: Feminism and Eve Ensler's Vagina Monologues" in *Signs: A Journal of Women and Culture* vol. 32 3 (2007) 727–758.

Crenshaw, Kimberlé, *Demarginalizing the Intersection of Race and Sex: A Black Feminist Critique of Anti-Discrimination Doctrine, Feminist Theory, and Anti-Racist Politic.* (University of Chicago Legal Forum, 1989).

Crenshaw, Kimberlé, "Mapping the Margins: Intersectionality, Feminism, and Violence Against Women" in *Stanford Law Review* vol. 43 6 (1991).

Crow, Barbara A. (ed.), *Radical Feminism: A Documentary Reader* (New York University Press, 2000).

Dines, Gail, Russo Ann, and Bob Jenson, *Pornography: The Production and Consumption of Inequality* (Routledge, 1997).

Donovan, Josephine, *Feminist Theory: The Intellectual Traditions* (Bloomsbury Academic, 2000).

Echols, Alice, *Daring to be Bad: Radical Feminism in America 1967–1975* (University of Minnesota Press, 1984).

Ensler, Eve, *The Vagina Monologues* (Dramatists Play Service, 2000).

Evans, Sara, *Personal Politics: The Roots of Women's Liberation in the Civil Rights Movement and the New Left* (Knopf Publishers, 1979).

Farquar, Mary and Chris Berry, "Speaking Bitterness: History, Media and Nation in Twentieth Century China" in *Historiography East and West* vol. 2 1 (2004) 116–143.

Ferguson, Ann, *Sexual Democracy: Women, Oppression, and Revolution* (Routledge, 1991).

Ferguson, Michaele, "Vulnerability by Marriage: Okin's Radical Feminist Critique of Structural Gender Inequality" in *Hypatia* vol. 31 3 (2016) 687–203.

Firestone, Shulamith, *The Dialectic of Sex: The Case for Feminist Revolution* (Bantam Books, 1970).

Federici, Sylvia and Jill Richards, "Every Woman is a Working Woman," *Boston Review*, December 19, 2018. https://www.bostonreview.net/articles/every-woman-working-woman/

Giddings, Paula, *When and Where I Enter: The Impact of Black Women on Race and Sex in America* (William and Morrow, 1984).

Grewal, Inderpal and Caren Kaplan (eds.), *Scattered Hegemonies* (University of Minnesota Press, 1994).

Haraway, Donna, *Simians, Cyborgs and Women: The Reinvention of Nature* (Routledge, 1991).

Hartsock, Nancy, *Money, Sex and Power: Toward a Feminist Historical Materialism* (Northeastern University Press, 1985).

Hasday, Jill Elaine, "Contest and Consent: A Legal History of Marital Rape" in *California Law Review* vol. 88 5 (2000).

Henley, Nancy M. and Clara Mayo (eds.), *Gender and Non-Verbal Behavior* (Springer-Verlag, 1981).

Hewitt, Nancy, "From Seneca Falls to Suffrage: Reimagining a Master Narrative in US Women's History" in Nancy Hewitt (ed.), *No Permanent Waves* (De Gruyter Press, 2010).

Hirshman, Linda, "Homeward Bound." *The American Prospect*, November 21, 2005.

hooks, bell, *Ain't I a Woman? Black Women and Feminism* (Pluto Press, 1982).

Hull, Gloria, Barbara Smith, and Patricia Bell Scott (eds.), *All the Men are Black, All the Women are White, but Some of Us are Brave* (The Feminist Press at CUNY, 1993).

Jaggar, Allison, *Feminist Politics and Human Nature* (Rowman and Allenheld/Harvester, 1983).

King, Deborah, "Multiple Jeopardy, Multiple Consciousness: The Context of a Black Feminist Ideology" in *Signs: A Journal of Women and Culture* vol. 14 1 (1988) 42–72.

Lorde, Audre, "The Master's Tools Will Never Dismantle the Master's House" in *Sister Outsider: Essays and Speeches* (Crossing Press, 1984).

MacKinnon, Catharine, *The Sexual Harassment of Working Women* (Harvard University Press, 1986).

MacKinnon, Catharine, *Feminism Unmodified* (Harvard University Press, 1988).

Marzo, Lori, "Feminism's Quest for Common Desires" in *Perspectives in Politics* vol. 8 1 (2010).

Mohanty, Chandra and Biddy Martin, "What's Home Got to Do with It?" in Chandra Mohanty (ed.) *Feminism Without Borders: Decolonizing Theory, Practicing Solidarity* (Duke University Press, 2003).

Moynihan, Daniel Patrick, *The Negro Family: The Case for National Action* (Office of Policy Planning and Research, United States Department of Labor, 1965).

Nash, Jennifer, "Rethinking Intersectionality" in *Feminist Review* vol. 89 1 (2008) 1–15.

Nicholson, Linda, *Gender and History: The Limits of Social Criticism in the Age of the Family* (Columbia University Press, 1985).

Nussbaum, Martha, *The Future of Feminist Liberalism* (Proceedings and Addresses of the American Philosophical Association, 2000). http://www.jstor.com/stable/3219683

Okin, Susan Muller, *Justice, Gender, and the Family* (Basic Books, 1991).

Phelan, Shane, "The Jargon of Authenticity: Adorno and Feminist Essentialism" in *Philosophy and Social Criticism* vol. 16 1 (1990) 39–54.

Pratt, Minnie Bruce, *Yours in Struggle* (Long Haul Press, 1984).

Reagon, Bernice Johnson, "Coalition Politics: Turning the Century" in Barbara Smith (ed.) *Home Girls: A Black Feminist Anthology* (Rutgers University Press, 1981).

Rich, Adrienne, "Compulsory Heterosexuality and Lesbian Existence" in *Blood, Bread and Poetry* (Norton Press, 1986).

Rich, Adrienne, *Of Woman Born: Motherhood as Experience and Institution* (Norton Press, 1995).

Rubin, Gayle "The Traffic in Women: Toward a Political Economy of Sex" in Rayna Reitner (ed.), *Toward an Anthropology of Women* (Monthly Review Press, 1975).

Russell, Diane H., *Rape in Marriage* (Indiana University Press, 1990).

Snitow, Ann, Christine Stansell, and Sharon Thompson, *Powers of Desire: The Politics of Sexuality* (Monthly Review Press, 1983).

Spivak, Gayatri, "Can the Subaltern Speak?" in Cary Nelson and Lawrence Grossberg (eds.), *Marxism and the Interpretation of Culture* (Macmillan Education, 1988) 271–313.

Tong, Rosemary, *Feminist Thought: A More Comprehensive Introduction* (Westview Press, 2009).

Vance, Carol (ed.), *Pleasure and Danger: Exploring Female Sexuality* (Pandora, 1989).

Wallace, Michelle, *Black Macho and the Myth of the Superwoman* (Doubleday, 1978).

Ware, Celestine, *Woman Power: The Movement for Women's Liberation* (Tower Publications, 1970).

Weigel, Moira, "Feminist Cyborg Donna Haraway: 'The Disorder of Our Era Isn't Necessary,'" *The Guardian*, June 20, 2019. https://www.theguardian.com/world/2019/jun/20/donna-haraway-interview-cyborg-manifesto-post-truth

Yamatta-Taylor, Keeanga, *How We Get Free: Black Feminism and the Combahee River Collective* (Haymarket Books, 2017).

Young, Iris, "The Ideal of Community and the Politics of Difference" in *Social Theory and Practice* vol. 12 1 (1986).

INDEX

For Product Safety Concerns and Information please contact our EU
representative GPSR@taylorandfrancis.com
Taylor & Francis Verlag GmbH, Kaufingerstraße 24, 80331 München, Germany